NATHAN GALE

TYPE 1

DIGITAL TYPEFACE DESIGN

LAURENCE KING PUBLISHING

LAURENCE KING

ACKNOWLEDGMENTS

Typography: Foundry Monoline, supplied by The Foundry

Thanks to all contributors/Cornel Windlin, Stephan Mueller and Julian Morey for their help and advice/ Jeremy Tankard for all PC conversions, building the installer and further advice for the Type 1 CD/ Helen Walters and all at Creative Review/Jo Lightfoot

A special thanks to Emma

FBRS

Published in 2002 by Laurence King Publishing Ltd

71 Great Russell Street
London WC1B 3BP
T +44 20 7430 8850
F +44 20 7430 8880
enquiries@laurenceking.co.uk
www.laurenceking.co.uk

A catalogue record for this book is available from the British Library.

ISBN 1 85669 270 1

Printed in Hong Kong

CONTENTS

CLASSIFICATION
This book uses typeface style for its broad chapter categories, using the primary characteristics of each design as the basis for classification.

TEXT
Typefaces for use as either body type or as display matter.

GRAPHIC
Typefaces of a vividly illustrative, pictorial or decorative design.

CALLIGRAPHIC
Hand-drawn types including scripts and faces that imitate handwriting.

DIRTY
Letterforms with processed, distressed or random elements.

STENCIL
Typefaces that resemble stencil letters cut from metal, paper etc.

LINE
Letters formed with the use of lines, including outline and inline.

MODULAR
Typefaces that use a standardized unit of construction.

BITMAPPED
Fonts based on the pixellated representation of type on screen.

INFORMATION
Each typeface is displayed showing a complete A to Z, in both upper- and lowercase, and 1 to 0 where possible. A display sentence has also been set, again in upper- and lowercase where possible, to show all characters in use. In the family list, alternate versions of typeface styles, such as italics, are shown in the display weight only. All typefaces are listed alphabetically within each chapter, indicated by the two reversed-out characters in the bottom right corner of each page.

The following data has been included with each typeface:

1 Name of designer/designers.
2 Name of company/foundry.
Where relevant, both company and foundry name are listed. Related foundries are listed where possible.
3 Location of designer/foundry.
Location of the designer or foundry that submitted the work.
4 Date of typeface design.

INTRODUCTION

Type 1 collects together digital typefaces from around the world, providing a unique visual resource in design and research for typographers and graphic designers.

The work featured was chosen by the editor: entries were selected from submissions sent in by designers in response to an invitation to submit work of their own choice.

Type 1 displays a selection of digital typeface design from the past thirteen years. Overall, the content of the book has been made as contemporary as possible, though some earlier, less known typeface designs have also been included. Future editions of the book will be time specific, only featuring typefaces designed since the publication of the previous edition.

Accompanying the book is a CD containing eight free fonts, one to represent each section of the book. These were exclusively commissioned from selected typeface designers and each is displayed at the beginning of the relevant chapter.

Nathan Gale, Editor

Type 1 CD typeface designers:

TEXT AMINTA
Gareth Hague, Alias, UK
GRAPHIC METROPOLIS
Christian Küsters, Acme Fonts, UK
CALLIGRAPHIC DIET
Shin Sasaki, Extra Design, Japan
DIRTY JOHNHADANIGHTMARE(LASTNIGHT)
Chester, Thirstype, US
STENCIL ASPHALT
Masahiko Nakamura, Lineto, Switzerland
LINE CIRCUIT
David Rust, Optimo, Switzerland
MODULAR STUDIO
Tom Hingston Studio, UK
BITMAPPED BASIC-21
Julian Morey, Club Twenty-One, UK

TYPE 1 FONT CRATER
Nathan Gale, UK

All fonts are PostScript, Macintosh/PC compatible.

AMINTA

AMINTA

AaBbCcDdEeFfGgHhIi
JjKkLlMmNnOoPpQqRr
SsTtUuVvWwXxYyZz
1234567890

AMINTA

The quick brown fox jumps over the lazy dog
THE QUICK BROWN FOX JUMPS OVER THE LAZY DOG

AMINTA FAMILY

Aminta

Gareth Hague
Alias
London, UK
2001

Aminta was designed specially
for TYPE 1 and is free on the CD
that accompanies this book. It mixes
the utilitarian aesthetic of Courier
with the expressive and intuitive
letterforms derived from drawing
and handwriting.

AMINTA

ALPHA HEADLINE

ALPHA HEADLINE

AABCDEFGGHIIKK
LMNOPQQRRSTUVV
WWXXYYZ
1234567890

ALPHA HEADLINE

THE QUICK BROWN FOX JUMPS OVER THE LAZY DOG
THE QUICK BROWN FOX JUMPS OVER THE LAZY DOG

ALPHA HEADLINE FAMILY

ALPHA HEADLINE

Cornel Windlin
Lineto
Zurich, Switzerland
1993/1997

Alpha Headline is derived from standard British car registration plates. The first version dates back to 1991.

ALPHA HEADLINE

ALPHAPEG

ALPHAPEG
ABCDEFGHIJKLMNOP
QRSTUVWXYZ
1234567890

ALPHAPEG

THE QUICK BROWN FOX JUMPS OVER THE LAZY DOG

ALPHAPEG FAMILY

ALPHAPEG
ALPHAPEG MONO

David Crow
Stockport, UK
2001

Alphapeg was inspired by a box of plastic menu board letters found at Liverpool Art School. The letters were digitized and then optically adjusted for legibility while retaining their original character.

ALPHAPEG

ALPINE

alpine

abcdefghijklmnopq

rsttuvwxyz

1234567890

ALPINE

the quick brown fox jumps over the lazy dog

ALPINE FAMILY

alpine

Julian Morey
Club Twenty-One
London, UK
2000

Alpine was based on an unused masthead redesign for a men's fashion magazine, and takes much of its inspiration from 1970s Dutch modernism.

ALPINE

ANTHROPOLYMORPHICS 2.0 S

ANTHROPOLYMORPHICS

AaBbCcDdEeFfGgHhIiJjKkLl
MmNnOoPpQqRrSsTtUuVv
WwXxYyZz
1234567890

ANTHROPOLYMORPHICS 2.0 S

The quick brown fox jumps over the lazy dog
THE QUICK BROWN FOX JUMPS OVER THE LAZY DOG

ANTHROPOLYMORPHICS FAMILY

Anthropolymorphics 1.0 R
Anthropolymorphics 1.1 R
Anthropolymorphics 2.0 S
Anthropolymorphics 2.1 S

Matius Gerardo Grieck
[+ism]
London, UK
2000

Anthropolymorphics is the fusion in both name and meaning of Anthroposophy and Polymorphism. The system of construction emphasizes individual character idiosyncrasies which, once set in text, integrate as a whole.

ANTHROPOLYMORPHICS 2.0 S

FOUNDRY ARCHITYPE BAYER

bayer

abcdeffgghijjkklmnop
qrsttuvwxyz
1234567890

FOUNDRY ARCHITYPE BAYER

the quick brown fox jumps over the lazy dog
the quick brown fox jumps over the lazy dog

FOUNDRY ARCHITYPE BAYER FAMILY

bayer

David Quay/Freda Sack
The Foundry
London, UK
1996

Foundry Architype Bayer has been drawn from Bauhaus-Archiv original sketches for a minimal sans serif typeface, with no capital letters, produced by Herbert Bayer in 1925.

FOUNDRY ARCHITYPE BAYER

BDR MONO

BDR MONO

AABC<DEEFFGHIↃ
KLMNOPQQRↃQSSTU
VWXYZZ
1234567890

BDR MONO

THE QUICK BROWN FOX JUMPS OVER THE LAZY DOG
THE QUICK BROWN FOX JUMPS OVER THE LAZY DOG

BDR MONO FAMILY

BDR MONO

Lopetz
Büro Destruct
Bern, Switzerland
1999

BDR Mono was intended as a new kind of OCR (Optical Character Recognition) typeface, hence the three letters in the name. It is monospaced and contains an alternative uppercase instead of lowercase characters .

BDR MONO

BD

BLISS EXTRA LIGHT

BLISS

AaBbCcDdEeFfGgHhIiJj

KkLlMmNnOoPpQqRrSs

TtUuVvWwXxYyZz

1234567890

BLISS EXTRA LIGHT

The quick brown fox jumps over the lazy dog
THE QUICK BROWN FOX JUMPS OVER THE LAZY DOG

BLISS FAMILY

Bliss Extra Light
Bliss Extra Light Italic
BLISS EXTRA LIGHT SMALL CAPS
BLISS EXTRA LIGHT SMALL CAPS ITALIC
Bliss Light
Bliss Regular
Bliss Medium
Bliss Bold
Bliss Extra Bold
Bliss Heavy

Jeremy Tankard
Jeremy Tankard Typography
London, UK
1996/2001

Bliss was developed after a study of five typefaces: Gill Sans, Edward Johnston's Underground typeface, Syntax, Frutiger and Jock Kinneir's Transport typeface. It was intended to be the first commercial typeface with an English feel since Gill Sans.

BLISS EXTRA LIGHT

BREMNER REGULAR

BREMNER

AaBbCcDdEeFfGgHhIiJj
KkLlMmNnOoPpQqRrSs
TtUuVvWwXxYyZz
1234567890

BREMNER REGULAR

The quick brown fox jumps over the lazy dog
THE QUICK BROWN FOX JUMPS OVER THE LAZY DOG

BREMNER FAMILY

Bremner Light
Bremner Regular
Bremner Bold

Adrian Talbot
Intro
London, UK
2000

Bremner was created for the redesign of Mute Records' visual identity. It was inspired by Herbert Bayer, the Bauhaus and the Modernist design movement.

BREMNER REGULAR

AF CARPLATES BOLD

CARPLATES

AaBbCcDdEeFfGgHhIi

JjKkLlMmNnOoPpQqRr

SsTtUuVvWwXxYyZz

1234567890

AF CARPLATES BOLD

The quick brown fox jumps over the lazy dog
THE QUICK BROWN FOX JUMPS OVER THE LAZY DOG

AF CARPLATES FAMILY

Carplates Medium
Carplates Bold

Concept/uppercase letters:
Sandy Suffield
Lowercase letters:
Christian Küsters
Acme Fonts
London, UK
1997

AF Carplates is based on the standard UK licence plate typeface. The concepts of context and generic use were the inspiration.

AF CARPLATES BOLD

COURIER SANS REGULAR

COURIER SANS

AaBbCcDdEeFfGgHh
IiJjKkLlMmNnOoPpQq
RrSstuVvWwXxYyZz
1234567890

COURIER SANS REGULAR

The quick brown fox jumps over the lazy dog
THE QUICK BROWN FOX JUMPS OVER THE LAZY DOG

COURIER SANS FAMILY

Courier Sans Light
Courier Sans Regular
Courier Sans Bold

James Goggin
Lineto
Zurich, Switzerland
1994

Courier Sans was originally designed during the first year of Goggin's graphic design degree. By taking the generic Macintosh system font and cutting off all the serifs, a pleasantly anonymous and functional sans serif was created.

COURIER SANS REGULAR

CRAYFISH ROUNDED

crayfish rounded

abcdefghijklmnopq
rstuvwxyz
123456789

CRAYFISH ROUNDED

the quick brown fox jumps over the lazy dog

CRAYFISH ROUNDED FAMILY

crayfish rounded

Simon Gofton
Tom Hingston Studio
London, UK
2001

Crayfish Rounded is a lowercase font drawn specifically for the band Spacek. It was initially intended as a stand-alone logotype but was subsequently developed for use throughout the single and album sleeve campaign as a display font.

CRAYFISH ROUNDED

CR GOTHIC BOLD

CR GOTHIC

ABCDEFGHIJKLMN
OPQRSTUVWXYZ
1234567890

CR GOTHIC BOLD

THE QUICK BROWN FOX JUMPS OVER THE LAZY DOG

CR GOTHIC FAMILY

CR GOTHIC
CR GOTHIC BOLD

Art Direction: Nathan Gale
Design: Robin Nicholas
AGFA Monotype
Redhill, UK
2000

CR Gothic was drawn specifically for use within Creative Review magazine. Based around Franklin Gothic, it has been carefully redrawn to eliminate the strong thick to thin contrast, and incorporates a new style 'G'.

CR GOTHIC BOLD

DETROIT MM 500 WEIGHT 500 OPTICAL

DETROIT MM

AaBbCcDdEeFfGgHhIi

JjKkLlMmNnOoPpQqRr

SsTtUuVvWwXxYyZz

1234567890

DETROIT MM 500 WEIGHT 500 OPTICAL

The quick brown fox jumps over the lazy dog
THE QUICK BROWN FOX JUMPS OVER THE LAZY DOG

DETROIT MM FAMILY

Detroit MM 0 0
Detroit MM 0 1000
Detroit MM 500 500
Detroit MM 1000 0
Detroit MM 1000 1000

Stephane Delgado/
Gilles Gavillet/David Rust
Optimo
Lausanne, Switzerland
1997

Detroit MM allows the user to modify the shape and the weight of the font using Multiple Master technology. It was designed at Cranbrook Academy of Art in Detroit, Michigan.

DETROIT MM 500 WEIGHT 500 OPTICAL

DIALOGUE

dialogue

AϾbıczdɛpfɔɐɣhıi̅]n
klɹ]mψnnσȯpϙqɾsɹ
ʃxʍıvʍxɒyʊzɪ

DIALOGUE

עۿ ซʊwɭ kıa ɾqhσ zɸʍɭɒɹ nσɔ mɒsɾŋ lɀʊɪɒ kıɟ
the quick brown fσx Jumps σvɛr the lazy dσg

DIALOGUE FAMILY

dialogue

David Crow/Yaki Molcho
Stockport, UK
1999

Dialogue's starting point was a visit to the School of Design Studies in Tel Aviv, where most of the public information is displayed in Hebrew and English. The aim was to design a font that could display these two languages in harmony.

DIALOGUE

DIM REGULAR

DIM

AaBbCcDdEeFfGgHhIiJjKkLlMmNn
OoPpQqRrSsTtUuVvWwXxYyZz
1234567890

DIM REGULAR

The quick brown fox jumps over the lazy dog
THE QUICK BROWN FOX JUMPS OVER THE LAZY DOG

DIM FAMILY

Dim Slim
Dim Regular

Tim Fletcher
Typical
London, UK
1997

Dim is a reduction of Din Engschrift to its simplest form. All elements considered unnecessary have been removed to produce a stripped-down, minimal typeface.

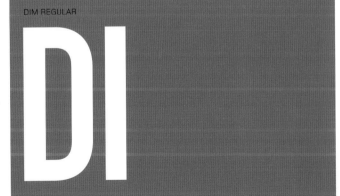

DIM REGULAR

EIDETIC NEO REGULAR

EIDETIC

AaBbCcDdEeFfGgHhIi
JjKkLlMmNnOoPpQqRr
SsTtUuVvWwXxYyZz
1234567890

EIDETIC NEO REGULAR

The quick brown fox jumps over the lazy dog
THE QUICK BROWN FOX JUMPS OVER THE LAZY DOG

EIDETIC FAMILY

Eidetic Neo Regular
Eidetic Neo Italic
EIDETIC NEO SMALL CAPS
eidetic neo omni
Eidetic Neo Bold
Eidetic Neo Black

Rodrigo Cavazos
Psy/Ops Type Foundry
Emigre Inc.
San Francisco, US
1998/2000

Eidetic features a fairly traditional, neoclassical foundation which also incorporates balanced, non-classical proportions and subtle traces of deconstruction.

EIDETIC NEO REGULAR

EUNUVERSE ROMAN

EUNUVERSE

AaBbCcDdEeFfGgHhIi

JjKkLIMmNnOoPpQqRr

SsTtUuVvWwXxYyZz

1234567890

EUNUVERSE ROMAN

The quick brown fox jumps over the lazy dog
THE QUICK BROWN FOX JUMPS OVER THE LAZY DOG

EUNUVERSE FAMILY

Eunuverse Roman
Eunuverse Italic
Eunuverse Bold
Eunuverse Extra Bold

Barry Deck
Thirstype
Barrington, US
1998

Eunuverse was designed exclusively for use in Ray Gun magazine when Barry Deck was art director in the late 1990s. The clean sans serif characters are reminiscent of Adrian Frutiger's Univers type family in both form and proportion.

EUNUVERSE ROMAN

FOUNDRY GRIDNIK REGULAR

GRIDNIK

AaBbCcDdEeFfGgHhIi
JjKkLlMmNnOoPpQqRr
SsTtUuVvWwXxYyZz
1234567890

FOUNDRY GRIDNIK REGULAR

The quick brown fox jumps over the lazy dog
THE QUICK BROWN FOX JUMPS OVER THE LAZY DOG

FOUNDRY GRIDNIK FAMILY

Gridnik Light
Gridnik Regular
Gridnik Medium
Gridnik Bold

David Quay/Freda Sack
with Wim Crouwel
The Foundry
London, UK
1998

Foundry Gridnik derives from a typeface created by Dutch designer Wim Crouwel in the late 1960s. Crouwel was often affectionately referred to as 'Mr Gridnik' by his contemporaries because of his devotion to grid systems.

FOUNDRY GRIDNIK REGULAR

GRIFFITH GOTHIC BLACK

GRIFFITH GOTHIC

AaBbCcDdEeFfGgHhIiJj

KkLlMmNnOoPpQqRrSs

TtUuVvWwXxYyZz

1234567890

GRIFFITH GOTHIC BLACK

The quick brown fox jumps over the lazy dog
THE QUICK BROWN FOX JUMPS OVER THE LAZY DOG

GRIFFITH GOTHIC FAMILY

Griffith Gothic Thin
Griffith Gothic Light
Griffith Gothic Regular
Griffith Gothic Bold
Griffith Gothic Black
Griffith Gothic Black Italic
Griffith Gothic Condensed Black
Griffith Gothic Ultra

Tobias Frere-Jones
Font Bureau
Boston, US
1997/1999

Griffith Gothic is a revival of the typeface Bell Gothic, designed by C.H.Griffith in 1937. It retains the original's thinning of joints as a salient feature. Italics and condensed versions complete this legible sans series.

GRIFFITH GOTHIC BLACK

HOBOKEN HIGH SLAB

HOBOKEN HIGH

AaBbCcDdEeFfGgHhIi
JjKkLlMmNnOoPpQqRr
SsTtUuVvWwXxYyZz
1234567890

HOBOKEN HIGH SLAB

The quick brown fox jumps over the lazy dog
THE QUICK BROWN FOX JUMPS OVER THE LAZY DOG

HOBOKEN HIGH FAMILY

Hoboken High Sans
Hoboken High Slab

Nico Schweizer
Lineto
Zurich, Switzerland
1998

Hoboken High's twin fonts were based on the lettering commonly used on sports jerseys and uniforms in the United States.

HOBOKEN HIGH SLAB

INGENIEUR REGULAR

INGENIEUR

AaBbCcDdEeFfGgHhIiJj
KkLeMmNnOoPpQqRrSsTt
UuVuWwXxYyZ3
1234567890

INGENIEUR REGULAR

The quick brown fox jumps over the eazy dog
THE QUICK BROWN FOX JUMPS OVER THE LAZY DOG

INGENIEUR FAMILY

Ingenieur Extra Light
Ingenieur Uetra Light
Ingenieur Light
Ingenieur Regular
Ingenieur Medium
Ingenieur Boed
Ingenieur Black

Niels Wehrspann
//copy//
Lausanne, Switzerland
1999

Ingenieur is a geometric typeface inspired by a fascination with low-tech fonts such as those on shop windows and street signs. These fonts are often designed by engineers unfamiliar with the craft of typeface design.

INGENIEUR REGULAR

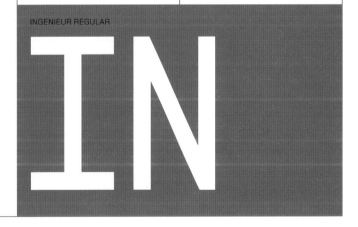

JUDE

AaBbCcDdEeFfGgHhIi
JjKkLlMmNnOoPpQqRr
SsTtUuVvWwXxYyZz
1234567890

JUDE MEDIUM

The quick brown fox jumps over the lazy dog
THE QUICK BROWN FOX JUMPS OVER THE LAZY DOG

JUDE FAMILY

Jude Light
Jude Medium
Jude Medium Italic
Jude Bold
Jude Black

Gareth Hague
Alias
London, UK
1999

Jude's simple, angular and sharp-edged letterforms were created using the geometric precision of the computer. Classical references were avoided to produce a bold, modern serif typeface for text and display.

JUDE MEDIUM

AF KLAMPENBORG BOLD

KLAMPENBORG

AaBbCcDdEeFfGgHhIiJj
KkLlMmNnOoPpQqRrSsTt
UuVvWwXxYyZz
1234567890

AF KLAMPENBORG BOLD

The quick brown fox jumps over the lazy dog
THE QUICK BROWN FOX JUMPS OVER THE LAZY DOG

AF KLAMPENBORG FAMILY

Klampenborg Regular
Klampenborg Medium
Klampenborg Bold

Henrik Kubel/Scott Williams
A2–Graphics/SW/HK
fontyoufonts.com/Acme Fonts
London, UK
1997/1999

AF Klampenborg was designed for sign systems and display text. The cut corners enable very tight spacing, allowing more letters per line. It also works well in small sizes where it looks clean and structured without being mechanical.

AF KLAMPENBORG BOLD

LUTZ HEADLINE

LUTZ HEADLINE

AABCDEFGGHIIJJ
KKLMMNOPQRRSTU
VVWWXXYYZ
1234567890

LUTZ HEADLINE

THE QUICK BROWN FOX JUMPS OVER THE LAZY DOG
THE QUICK BROWN FOX JUMPS OVER THE LAZY DOG

LUTZ HEADLINE FAMILY

LUTZ HEADLINE

Cornel Windlin
Lineto
Zurich, Switzerland
1993/1997

Lutz Headline, like Alpha Headline, is derived from an anonymous design for British car registration plates.

LUTZ HEADLINE

ARS MAQUETTE BLACK

MAQUETTE

AaBbCcDdEeFfGgHhIi
JjKkLlMmNnOoPpQqRr
SsTtUuVvWwXxYyZz
1234567890

ARS MAQUETTE BLACK

The quick brown fox jumps over the lazy dog
THE QUICK BROWN FOX JUMPS OVER THE LAZY DOG

ARS MAQUETTE FAMILY

Maquette Light
Maquette Regular
Maquette Medium
Maquette Bold
Maquette Black

Angus R. Shamal
ARS Type
Amsterdam, The Netherlands
1999/2000

ARS Maquette is a humanistic typeface, designed for small text sizes as well as for headline applications. The idea was to keep it clean and invisible when used within the framework of a design, while maintaining its distinctive character.

ARS MAQUETTE BLACK

METSYS BOLD

METSYS

AaßbCcDdEeFfGgHhIi
JjKkLlMmNnOoPpQqRr
SsTtUuVvWwXxYyZz
1234567890

METSYS BOLD

The quick brown fox jumps over the lazy dog
THE QUICK BROWN FOX JUMPS OVER THE LAZY DOG

METSYS FAMILY

Metsys Thin
Metsys Light
Metsys Medium
Metsys Bold
Metsys Black

David James/Gareth Hague
Alias
London, UK
1997

Metsys, derived from a logotype designed for electronic band System 7, is a different take on the monoline aesthetic. Letterforms are purified, rounded, almost abstract graphic shapes.

METSYS BOLD

FE MITTELSCHRIFT

MITTELSCHRIFT

AaBbCcDdEeFfGgHhIi
JjKkLlMmNnOoPpQqRr
SsTtUuVvWwXxYyZz
1234567890

FE MITTELSCHRIFT

The quick brown fox jumps over the lazy dog
THE QUICK BROWN FOX JUMPS OVER THE LAZY DOG

FE MITTELSCHRIFT FAMILY

Mittelschrift
Engschrift

Stephan Mueller
Lineto
Zurich, Switzerland
1995–1997

FE Mittelschrift was designed after the German government introduced a new typeface for car registration plates with the aim of making them impossible to counterfeit. This effort was swiftly undermined by the publication of this font.

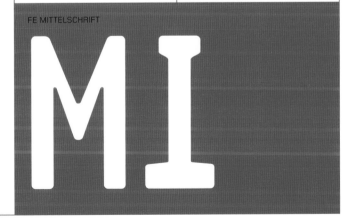

FE MITTELSCHRIFT

FOUNDRY MONOLINE REGULAR

MONOLINE

AaBbCcDdEeFfGgHhIi
JjKkLlMmNnOoPpQqRr
SsTtUuVvWwXxYyZz
1234567890

FOUNDRY MONOLINE REGULAR

The quick brown fox jumps over the lazy dog
THE QUICK BROWN FOX JUMPS OVER THE LAZY DOG

FOUNDRY MONOLINE FAMILY

Monoline Ultra Light
Monoline Light
Monoline Regular
Monoline Regular Italic
Monoline Medium
Monoline Bold

David Quay/Freda Sack
The Foundry
London, UK
2000

Foundry Monoline's clean, linear appearance was created using strong structural elements. Each character has its own subtleties, with a monoline appearance which has been achieved through careful optical adjustment.

FOUNDRY MONOLINE REGULAR

MO

NORMETICA A

NORMETICA

AaBbCcDdEeFfGgHhIi

JjKkLlMmNnOoPpQqRr

SsTtUuVvWwXxYyZz

1234567890

NORMETICA A

The quick brown fox jumps over the lazy dog
THE QUICK BROWN FOX JUMPS OVER THE LAZY DOG

NORMETICA FAMILY

Normetica A
Normetica B
Normetica C

Norm
Lineto
Zurich, Switzerland
1999

Normetica is a monospaced font designed to fit the grid of Norm magazine issue nr.0, a book and website exploring two and three-dimensional spaces and objects.

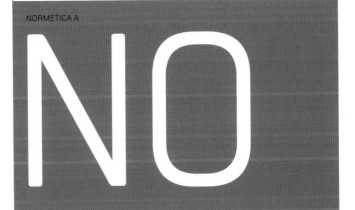

NORMETICA A

NUMBER TWO

NUMBER TWO

AaBbCcDdEeFfGgHhIiJjKkLlMm
NnOoPpQqRrSsTtUuVvWwXxYyZz
1234567890

NUMBER TWO

The quick brown fox jumps over the lazy dog
THE QUICK BROWN FOX JUMPS OVER THE LAZY DOG

NUMBER TWO FAMILY

Number Two

Martha Stuttergger
Lineto
Zurich, Switzerland
1996

Number Two was inspired by an early sans serif typeface called Berthold Schmale Runde Grotesk.

NUMBER TWO

OFFICE REGULAR

OFFICE

AaBbCcDdEeFfGgHhIi

JjKkLlMmNnOoPpQqRr

SsTtUuVvWwXxYyZz

1234567890

OFFICE REGULAR

The quick brown fox jumps over the lazy dog
THE QUICK BROWN FOX JUMPS OVER THE LAZY DOG

OFFICE FAMILY

Office Regular
Office Italic
Office Bold

Stephan Mueller
Lineto
Zurich, Switzerland
1999

Office, a monospaced text font, was developed from the designs of the Overseas typeface family. Overseas was based on a set of rubber stamps used for printing lettering on shipping containers and wooden boxes.

OFFICE REGULAR

OZ BLACK

Oz

AaBbCcDdEeFfGgHhIi
JjKkLlMmNnOoPpQqRr
SsTtUuVvWwXxYyZz
1234567890

OZ BLACK

The quick brown fox jumps over the lazy dog
THE QUICK BROWN FOX JUMPS OVER THE LAZY DOG

OZ FAMILY

Oz Regular
Oz Medium
Oz Bold
Oz Extra Bold
Oz Black
Oz Black Italic

Patrick Giasson
Thirstype
Barrington, US
1998/1999

Oz is a skilfully drawn and thoughtfully rendered revival of the Oswald family of type, created by Oswald Cooper in the 1920s.

OZ BLACK

PACIFIC REGULAR

PACIFIC

ABCDEFGHIJKLMNOP
QRSTUVWXYZ
1234567890

PACIFIC REGULAR

THE QUICK BROWN FOX JUMPS OVER THE LAZY DOG

PACIFIC FAMILY

PACIFIC LIGHT
PACIFIC REGULAR
PACIFIC BOLD
PACIFIC BLACK

Julian Morey
Club Twenty-One
London, UK
1999

Pacific is an octic typeface design that was influenced by American naval lettering.

PACIFIC REGULAR

AF PAN BOLD

PAN

ABCDEFGHIJKLMN
OPQRSTUVWXYZ
1234567890

AF PAN BOLD

THE QUICK BROWN FOX JUMPS OVER THE LAZY DOG

AF PAN FAMILY

PAN REGULAR
PAN BOLD

Robert Green
Acme Fonts
London, UK
1996/1997

AF Pan is based on a typeface from the interface of old NatWest bank cash machines. It was inspired by the idea that the original had been drawn by a computer programmer rather than a type designer.

AF PAN BOLD

PENNSYLVANIA REGULAR

PENNSYLVANIA

AaBbCcDdEeFfGgHhIiJj

KkLlMmNnOoPpQqRrSsTt

UuVvWwXxYyZz

1234567890

PENNSYLVANIA REGULAR

The quick brown fox jumps over the lazy dog
THE QUICK BROWN FOX JUMPS OVER THE LAZY DOG

PENNSYLVANIA FAMILY

Pennsylvania Regular

Pennsylvania Italic

PENNSYLVANIA REGULAR SMALL CAPS

Pennsylvania Bold

Christian Schwartz
Font Bureau
Boston, US
1999/2000

Pennsylvania was inspired by the monospaced capitals and numbers on car licence plates in Pennsylvania.

PENNSYLVANIA REGULAR

ROLECKS

ROLECKS

ABCDEFGHIJKLMN

OPQRSTUVWXYZ

1234567890

ROLECKS

THE QUICK BROWN FOX JUMPS OVER THE LAZY DOG

ROLECKS FAMILY

ROLECKS

Gregor Schönborn
//copy//
Lausanne, Switzerland
2000

Rolecks is based on the logotype of Rolex, which was definitely not optimized for a full character typeface. Turning this logotype into an Egyptian font has created a punk typeface in total contrast to the logo's original purpose.

ROLECKS

RUBBER MEDIUM

RUBBER

AaBbCcDdEeFFGgHhIi
JjKkLlMmNnOoPpQqRr
SsTtUuVvWwXxYyZz
1234567890

RUBBER MEDIUM

The quick brown Fox jumps over the lazy dog
THE QUICK BROWN FOX JUMPS OVER THE LAZY DOG

RUBBER FAMILY

Rubber Small
Rubber Medium
Rubber Large
Rubber Ribbed

Sebastian Lester
GarageFonts
Silver Spring, US
2001

Rubber was inspired by the
popularity of blocky, square display
faces in the UK.

RUBBER MEDIUM

RUBDOWN REGULAR

RUBDOWN

AaBbCcDdEeFfGgHhIi
JjKkLlMmNnOoPpQqRr
SsTtUuVvWwXxYyZz
1234567890

RUBDOWN REGULAR

The quick brown fox jumps over the lazy dog
THE QUICK BROWN FOX JUMPS OVER THE LAZY DOG

RUBDOWN FAMILY

Rubdown Ultra Light
Rubdown Light
Rubdown Regular
Rubdown Medium
Rubdown Bold
Rubdown Black

Niels Wehrspann
//copy//
Lausanne, Switzerland
1999

Rubdown was digitized from a transfer sheet found in a local shop. The extreme weight changes to this monoline font were created with Multiple Master software.

RUBDOWN REGULAR

SCENE MEDIUM

SCENE

AaBbCcDdEeFfGgHhIi
JjKkLlMmNnOoPpQqRr
SsTtUuVvWwXxYyZz
1234567890

SCENE MEDIUM

The quick brown fox jumps over the lazy dog
THE QUICK BROWN FOX JUMPS OVER THE LAZY DOG

SCENE FAMILY

Scene Light
Scene Regular
Scene Medium
Scene Medium Italic
Scene Bold
Scene Black
Scene Ultra Black

Sebastian Lester
AGFA Monotype
Redhill, UK
2000/2001

Scene is a clean, calm, corporate typeface inspired by Boo Gothic, Din, Trade Gothic, News Gothic, Meta, and OCR-B.

SCENE MEDIUM

SC

SQUARE45 THIN

SQUARE45

AaBbCcDdEeFfGgHhIi
JjKkLIMmNnOoPpQqRr
SsTtUuVvWwXxYyZz
1234567890

SQUARE45 THIN

The quick brown fox jumps over the lazy dog
THE QUICK BROWN FOX JUMPS OVER THE LAZY DOG

SQUARE45 FAMILY

Square45 Thin
Square45 Thin Italic
Square40 Regular
Square40 Oblique
Square40 Outline

Carlos Segura/
Tnop Wangsillapakun
T–26 Digital Type Foundry
Chicago, US
2000

Square45 derives from Square40, a typeface designed in 1995 by Segura, which was based on the type from a 1940s propaganda sign.

SQUARE45 THIN

STORNO

STORNO

AaBbCcDdEeFfGgHhIi
JjKkLlMmNnOoPpQqRr
SsTtUuVvWwXxYyZz
1234567890

STORNO

The quick brown fox jumps over the lazy dog
THE QUICK BROWN FOX JUMPS OVER THE LAZY DOG

STORNO FAMILY

Storno

Elektrosmog
Lineto
Zurich, Switzerland
1999

Storno's upper- and lowercase are
interpretations of the numerals
from an old Sharp cash register.

STORNO

WDFB

WDFB

AaBbCcDdEeFfGgHhIiJj
KkLlMmNnOoPpQqRrSs
TtUuVvWwXxYyZz
1234567890

WDFB

The quick brown fox jumps over the lazy dog
THE QUICK BROWN FOX JUMPS OVER THE LAZY DOG

WDFB FAMILY

WDFB

Hideki Inaba
Hideki Inaba Design
Tokyo, Japan
2001

WDFB was created as a bespoke typeface for a children's clothing company in Japan.

WDFB

W'HAPPEN

WHAPPEN

AABCDEFGHIIJKL
MNOOPQQRSTUV
WWXYZ

W'HAPPEN

THE QUICK BROWN FOX JUMPS OVER THE LAZY DOG
THE QUICK BROWN FOX JUMPS OVER THE LAZY DOG

W'HAPPEN FAMILY

WHAPPEN
WHAPPEN STENCIL

Tom Hingston
Tom Hingston Studio
London, UK
2000

W'happen is based on an old
American woodcut typeface called
Poster Gothic. It was adapted and
redrawn as a headline font for a
fashion photography book.

W'HAPPEN

METROPOLIS

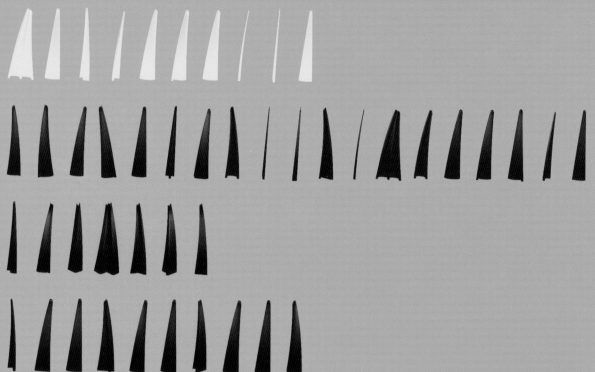

METROPOLIS

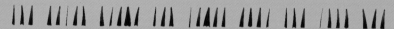

METROPOLIS USAGE

Concept and Art Direction:
Christian Küsters
3D Modelling: Paul Beavis
Acme Fonts
London, UK
2001

Metropolis was designed specially for TYPE 1 and is free on the CD that accompanies this book. It was designed as an experiment to explore a three-dimensional space on the two-dimensional surface of a page or screen.

METROPOLIS

FY 3D

FY 3D

FY 3D FAMILY

Henrik Kubel/Scott Williams
A2–Graphics/SW/HK
fontyoufonts.com
London, UK
2001

FY 3D is a grid-based typeface that
uses a simple optical effect. Each
character is constructed from two
alternative perspectives.

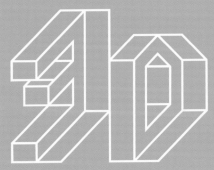

FY 3D

AF ANGEL

ANGEL

ABCDEFGHIJKLM
NOPQRSTUVWXYZ
1234567890

AF ANGEL

THE QUICK BROWN FOX JUMPS OVER THE LAZY DOG

AF ANGEL FAMILY

ANGEL

Christian Küsters
Acme Fonts
London, UK
1998

AF Angel was based on an old
woodblock typeface found in
Camberwell College of Arts, London.

AF ANGEL

BD ASCIIMAX

BD ASCIIMAX

BD ASCIIMAX FAMILY

Lopetz
Büro Destruct
Bern, Switzerland
1999

BD ASCIIMAX is inspired by ASCII art, graphic images composed of text. ASCII is the acronym for American Standard Code for Information Interchange. It's a set of 128 characters which are standard on almost all types of computer.

BD ASCIIMAX

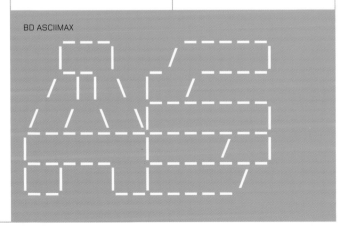

AUTOLOGIC

autologic

abcdefgahijklmno

parstuvwnuexxnz

1234567890

AUTOLOGIC

the quick brown fox jumps over the lazy dog
the quick brown fox jumps over the lazy dog

AUTOLOGIC FAMILY

autologic

Gilles Gavillet
Optimo
Lausanne, Switzerland
1997

Autologic was created to generate automatic logotypes and corporate identities without spending too much time and money.

AUTOLOGIC

F AUTOSUGGESTION

F AUTOSUGGESTION

F AUTOSUGGESTION FAMILY

Autosuggestion

Neville Brody
Fuse 9/FSI FontShop International
London, UK
1994

F Autosuggestion was created for
AutoFuse, the ninth issue of the
experimental type magazine Fuse.
It was formed from the negative
spaces of the typeface Blur, also
designed by Brody.

F AUTOSUGGESTION

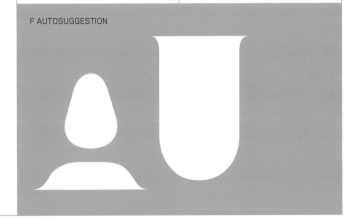

BIFF

BIFF

ABCDEFGHIJKLMN
OPQRSTUVWXYZ
1234567890

BIFF

THE QUICK BROWN FOX JUMPS OVER THE LAZY DOG

BIFF FAMILY

BIFF

Jonas Williamson
Lineto
Zurich, Switzerland
1999

Biff is inspired by early New York graffiti and its progression into throw-up styles, which were painted quickly with one layer of spray paint and an outline.

BIFF

BREAKDOWN

breakdown

abcdefghijklmno
pqrstuvwxyz
1234567890

BREAKDOWN

the quick brown fox jumps over the lazy dog

BREAKDOWN FAMILY

breakdown x
breakdown y
breakdown z
breakdown
breakup
breakthrough

Alexander Gelman
Design Machine
New York, US
1994

Breakdown was designed to utilize all three dimensions and contains three fonts representing x, y and z coordinates. When layered, these coordinates give the illusion of three-dimensional letterforms.

BREAKDOWN

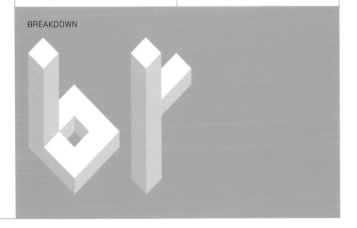

F CITY AVENUE

(alphabet specimen A–Z and numerals 1234567890 in F City Avenue typeface)

F CITY AVENUE

The quick brown fox jumps over the lazy dog
The quick brown fox jumps over the lazy dog

F CITY FAMILY

city architecture
city avenue
city
city skyline
city speed angst
city feedback

Neville Brody
Fuse 15/FSI FontShop International
London, UK
1997

F City was created for an issue of Fuse magazine based on the theme of cities. Its design draws on structural and emotional aspects of urban life and environment.

F CITY AVENUE

COINTRIN

COINTRIN

ABCDEFGHIJK
LMNOPQRSTUV
WXYZ
1234567890

COINTRIN

THE QUICK BROWN FOX JUMPS OVER THE LAZY DOG

COINTRIN FAMILY

COINTRIN

Kimou Meyer/Vincent Sahli
Grotesk
Geneva, Switzerland
1998

Cointrin was based on the old arrival and departure boards at Geneva airport.

COINTRIN

COLTRANE

COLTRANE

AaBbCcDdEeFfGgHhIiJjKkLlMm
NnOoPpQqRrSsTtUuVvWwXxYyZz
1234567890

COLTRANE

The quick brown fox jumps over the lazy dog
THE QUICK BROWN FOX JUMPS OVER THE LAZY DOG

COLTRANE FAMILY

Coltrane

Swifty
Swifty Typografix
London, UK
1994

Coltrane is a classic sixties font inspired by old John Coltrane record sleeves. An overweight typeface, it is best used at larger sizes to appreciate the extreme nature of its design.

COLTRANE

CUBICLE

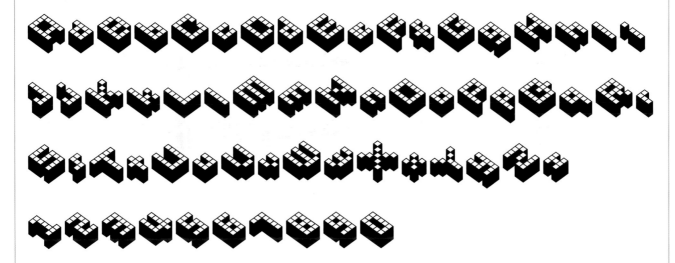

CUBICLE

CUBICLE FAMILY

**Nobutaka Sato/Shin Sasaki
Extra Design
Sapporo, Japan
1999**

Cubicle is an angled shadow version of the font Squaretype, also designed by Extra.

CUBICLE

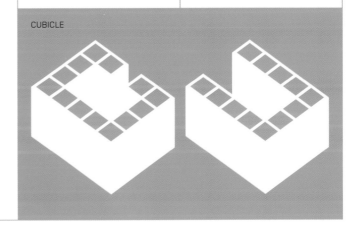

EAT LIGHTNING

EAT LIGHTNING

ABCDEEFFGHIIJJ
KLMNNOPPQRSTU
VWXYZ
1234567890

EAT LIGHTNING

THE QUICK BROWN FOX JUMPS OVER THE LAZY DOG
THE QUICK BROWN FOX JUMPS OVER THE LAZY DOG

EAT LIGHTNING FAMILY

EAT LIGHTNING

Mike Essl
The Chopping Block Inc.
New York, US
2001

Eat Lightning's inspiration came after hearing the line 'You're gonna eat lightning and you're gonna crap thunder' in the film Rocky. Designed at Cranbrook Academy of Art.

EAT LIGHTNING

EUPHORIC REGULAR

EUPHORIC

aabcodEeFgGg

HhiijKLmnopqq

RrsrtuvwxRyyz

1234567890

EUPHORIC REGULAR

The quick brown fox jumps over the lazy dog
THE QUICK BROWN FOX JUMPS OVER THE LAZY DOG

EUPHORIC FAMILY

Euphoric Thin
Euphoric regular
Euphoric regular italic
Euphoric Heavy
nuephoric Thin
nuephoric regular
nuephoric Heavy

Lee Basford/James Glover
Fluid
T-26 Digital Type Foundry/
Fountain
Birmingham, UK
1996

Euphoric was originally inspired by a paperclip style font in an old type specimen book. The design was initially used as a logotype, but was later developed into a full character set for T-26. Nuephoric is an updated square version of Euphoric.

EUPHORIC REGULAR

EXERCISE

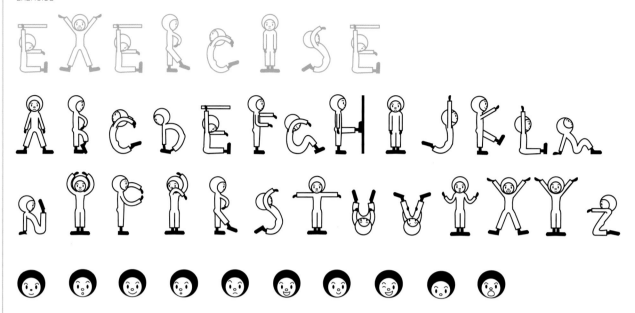

EXERCISE

THE QUICK BROWN FOX JUMPS OVER THE LAZY DOG

EXERCISE FAMILY

EXERCISE

Tomo Takeue
tomotomo.net
Tokyo, Japan
2000

Exercise was created for the
CodexTwo CD-Rom, published by
Matt Owens, and was inspired by the
need to be more healthy.

EXERCISE

FAT ULTRA

FAT ULTRA

AaBbCcDdEeFfGg

HhIiJjKkLlMmNn

PpQqRrSsTtUuWwXxYyZz

1234567890

FAT ULTRA

The quick brown fox jumps over the lazy dog
THE QUICK BROWN FOX JUMPS OVER THE LAZY DOG

FAT ULTRA FAMILY

Fat Ultra

ラフボ小につら

Nobutaka Sato
Extra Design
Sapporo, Japan
1998

Fat Ultra used the square as a starting point for each of its characters. Negative white space was then added to create the individual letterforms.

FAT ULTRA

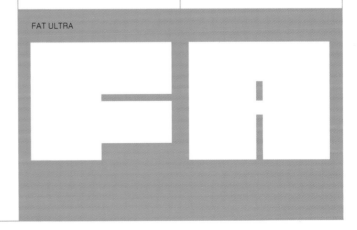

FLEXO MM 500 WEIGHT 500 OPTICAL

FLEXO MM

A a B b C C D d E e F f G g H h l i J j K k
L l M m N n D o P p Q q R r S s T t U u
U u W w X x Y y Z z
1 2 3 4 5 6 7 8 9 0

FLEXO MM 500 WEIGHT 500 OPTICAL

The quick brown fox jumps over the lazy dog
THE QUICK BROWN FOX JUMPS OVER THE LAZY DOG

FLEXO MM FAMILY

Flexo MM 500 500

FLEXO MM 1000 0

David Rust
Optimo
Lausanne, Switzerland
1998

Flexo MM allows the user to modify the shape and weight of the font using Multiple Master technology, adding a new playful and flexible dimension to typography, especially within the field of motion graphics.

FLEXO MM 500 WEIGHT 500 OPTICAL

FUNKADELIC

FUNKADELIC

AaBbCcDdEeFfGgHhIi
JjKkLlMmNnOoPpQqRr
SsTtUuVvWwXxYyZz
1234567890

FUNKADELIC

The quick brown fox jumps over the lazy dog
THE QUICK BROWN FOX JUMPS OVER THE LAZY DOG

FUNKADELIC FAMILY

Funkadelic

Swifty
Swifty Typografix
London, UK
1999

Funkadelic's sleek curves and clean
lines were inspired by seventies
sci-fi films such as Rollerball and
Death Race 2000.

FUNKADELIC

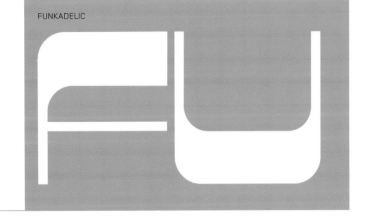

INTERFACER

INTERFACER

AaBbcɔdeɾɕqɕhIʋʋ
KᴋᴜLmᴘᴘnopɑqʀᴅ�̄ɕ
ʋʋɯɯxxʋɥʒʒ
1234567890

INTERFACER

ɘhɘ QuICK bROɯn ɾox ɟumᴘᴘ oʋɘR ɘhɘ LɑʒU doɕ
ɘhɘ QuICK bROɯn ɾox ɟumᴘᴘ oʋɘR ɘhɘ LɑʒU doɕ

INTERFACER FAMILY

Interfacer

Malte Haust
Bionic Systems
T–26 Digital Type Foundry
Düsseldorf, Germany
1998

Interfacer is an experiment in combining circles with letterforms. It was inspired by the rounded characters of the font Bauhaus.

INTERFACER

LINETO

LINETO

A a B b C c D d E e F f G g H h I i
J j K k L l M m N n O o P p Q q R r
S s T t U u V v W w X x Y y Z z
1 2 3 4 5 6 7 8 9 0

LINETO

The quick brown fox jumps over the lazy dog
THE QUICK BROWN FOX JUMPS OVER THE LAZY DOG

LINETO FAMILY

Lineto

Gilles Gavillet
Optimo
Lausanne, Switzerland
2001

Lineto was inspired by the type produced on Plotters, CAD printing machines.

LINETO

LINK

AaBbCcDdEeFfGgHhIiJj

KkLlMmNnOoPpQqRrSs

TtUuVvWwXxYyZz

1234567890

LINK

THE QUICK BROWN FOX JUMPS OVER THE LAZY DOG
The quick brown fox jumps over the lazy dog

LINK FAMILY

LINK

Megumu Kasuga
London, UK
1997

Link was originally designed as a corporate identity for a company in the Japanese music industry. Shapes from a bicycle chain were used to express Heavy Metal and Techno influences.

LINK

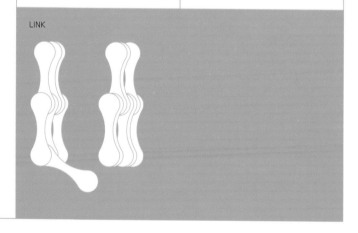

MYRNA

MYRNA

A a B b C c D d E e F f G g H h I i
J j K k L L M m N n O o P p Q q R r
S s T t U u V v W w X x Y y Z z
1 2 3 4 5 6 7 8 9 0

MYRNA

The quick brown fox jumps over the lazy dog
THE QUICK BROWN FOX JUMPS OVER THE LAZY DOG

MYRNA FAMILY

Myrna

Alexander Gelman/David Heasty
Design Machine
New York, US
2001

Myrna was designed as part of the new visual identity program for the Art Directors Club of New York. It was named to honour Myrna Davis, the club's Executive Director.

MYRNA

PANDERELLA MEDIUM

PANDERELLA

AaBbCcDdEeFFGgHhIiJj
KkLlMmNnOoPpQqRr
SsTtUuVvWwXxYyZz
1234567890

PANDERELLA MEDIUM

The quick brown Fox jumps over the lazy dog
THE QUICK BROWN FOX JUMPS OVER THE LAZY DOG

PANDERELLA FAMILY

Panderella Ultra Light
Panderella Light
Panderella Medium
Panderella Medium Italic
PANDERELLA MEDIUM CAPS
Panderella Bold
Panderella Heavy

Chester
Thirstype
Barrington, US
2000

Panderella was designed to pander
to the dance record sleeve and club
flyer design community.

PANDERELLA MEDIUM

PEZ

A B C D E E F F G H I I J K
L L M N N O P P Q R S S
T U V V W X Y Z
1 2 3 4 5 6 7 8 9 0

PEZ

THE QUICK BROWN FOX JUMPS OVER THE LAZY DOG
THE QUICK BROWN FOX JUMPS OVER THE LAZY DOG

PEZ FAMILY

PEZ

Laurent Benner
Lineto
Zurich, Switzerland
1999

Pez is derived from the three
letters in the logo of the famous
sweet dispensing toys.

PEZ

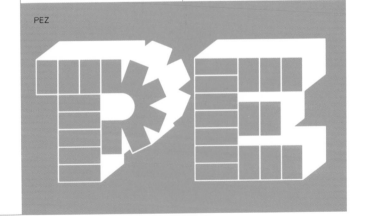

0062A PLOTTER

PLOTTER

Aa Bb Cc Dd Ee Ff Gg Hh

Ii Jj Kk Ll Mm Nn Oo Pp Qq Rr

Ss Tt Uu Vv Ww Xx Yy Zz

1234567890

0062A PLOTTER

The quick brown fox jumps over the lazy dog
THE QUICK BROWN FOX JUMPS OVER THE LAZY DOG

PLOTTER FAMILY

05a Plotter
025a Plotter
025b Plotter
0125a Plotter
0125b Plotter
0062a Plotter
0062a Plotter Bandzug
0062b Plotter
0031a Plotter
0031b Plotter

Wolfgang Breuer
Mittlere Körnung
forhomeorofficeuse.com
Frankfurt, Germany
1999

Plotter is the result of a typeface in a CAD program being gradually reduced in size to 0.031 of an inch.

0062A PLOTTER

FF POP

POP

AaBbCcDdEeFfGgHhIiJjKkLlMm
NnOoPpQqRrSsTtUuVvWwXxYyZz
1234567890

FF POP

The quick brown fox jumps over the lazy dog
THE QUICK BROWN FOX JUMPS OVER THE LAZY DOG

FF POP FAMILY

Pop

Pop Led

Neville Brody
FSI FontShop International
London, UK
1992

FF Pop was originally developed for a German music TV programme. Anticipating the need for fast moving but clearly identifiable credits, FF Pop was designed with sharply cut corners and arrowed edges on some of the characters.

FF POP

Q-BIC R/L

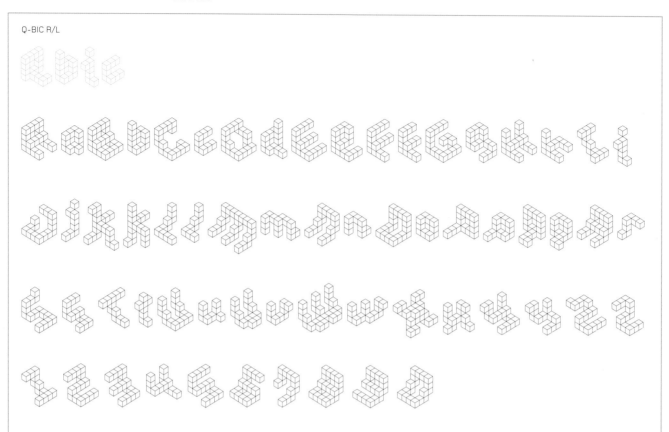

Q-BIC R/L

Q-BIC FAMILY

Megumu Kasuga
London, UK
2000

Q-bic was originally designed for an animated sequence in which an initial letterform transformed into various characters, spelling a word.

Q-BIC R

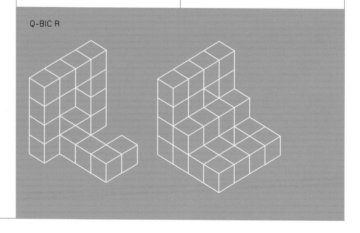

BD RAINBOW

RAINBOW

AaBbCcDdEeFfGgHhIiJj

KkLlMmNnOoPpQqRrSsTt

UuVvWwXxYyZz

1234567890

BD RAINBOW

The quick brown fox jumps over the lazy dog
THE QUICK BROWN FOX JUMPS OVER THE LAZY DOG

BD RAINBOW FAMILY

Rainbow

MBrunner/Lopetz
Büro Destruct
Bern, Switzerland
2000

BD Rainbow was originally a logotype for the Büro Destruct spin-off Rainbow, which is a project, concept and philosophy based on working without an office.

BD RAINBOW

RANGE BOLD

RANGE

AaBbCcDdEeFfGgHhIi
JjKkLlMmNnOoPpQqRr
SsTtUuVvWwXxYyZz
1234567890

RANGE BOLD

The quick brown fox jumps over the lazy dog
THE QUICK BROWN FOX JUMPS OVER THE LAZY DOG

RANGE FAMILY

Range Light
Range Medium
Range Bold
Range Extra Bold
Range Black

Rian Hughes
Device
London, UK
2000

Range is a modern font that evokes the computer aesthetic of OCR-A, but also functions as a fully kerned and readable font at both headline and body copy text sizes.

RANGE BOLD

BD RELAUNCH

RELAUNCH

ABCDEFGHIJJKKLL
MNOPQRRSSTTUU
WWXXYYZZ
1234567890

BD RELAUNCH

THE QUICK BROWN FOX JUMPS OVER THE LAZY DOG
THE QUICK BROWN FOX JUMPS OVER THE LAZY DOG

BD RELAUNCH FAMILY

RELAUNCH
リラーンチ

Lopetz
Büro Destruct
Bern, Switzerland
2000

BD Relaunch is based on part of a letterform taken from the font BD Rainbow. The katakana version, an angular form of Japanese kana, was designed by SavWo from Cyclone Graphics, Tokyo.

BD RELAUNCH

SPACER

SPACER

AABBCCDDEFFGGHHIIJJKK
LLMMNNOOPPQQRRSSTTUU
VVWWXXYYZZ
1234567890

SPACER

THE QUICK BROWN FOX JUMPS OVER THE LAZY DOG
THE QUICK BROWN FOX JUMPS OVER THE LAZY DOG

SPACER FAMILY

SPACER

Julian Morey
Club Twenty-One
London, UK
1999

Spacer was originally a drawing of
an unusual 1960s grotesque
typeface. The outlines were then
processed using the intersect filter
in FreeHand.

SPACER

FOUNDRY ARCHITYPE STEDELIJK

stedelijk

abcdefghijklmnopqrs
tuvwxyz
1234567890

FOUNDRY ARCHITYPE STEDELIJK

the quick brown fox jumps over the lazy dog

FOUNDRY ARCHITYPE STEDELIJK FAMILY

stedelijk

David Quay/Freda Sack
with Wim Crouwel
The Foundry
London, UK
1997

Foundry Architype Stedelijk is from
a collection of fonts developed by
The Foundry in close collaboration
with Wim Crouwel. It originally
appeared on one of Crouwel's
seminal posters for the Stedelijk
Museum in the late 1960s.

FOUNDRY ARCHITYPE STEDELIJK

BD TATAMI

BD TATAMI

The quick brown fox jumps over the lazy dog
THE QUICK BROWN FOX JUMPS OVER THE LAZY DOG

BD TATAMI FAMILY

Tatami

Lopetz
Büro Destruct
Bern, Switzerland
2001

BD Tatami was inspired by forms in
Japanese architecture and interior
design, including wooden roofs and
tatami mats.

BD TATAMI

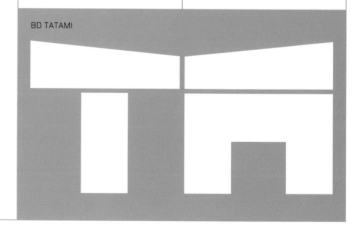

TETRA B BOLD

TETRA B

AaBbCcDdEeFfGgHhIi
JjKkLlMmNnOoPpQqRr
SsTtUuVvWwXxYyZz
1234567890

TETRA B BOLD

The quick brown fox jumps over the lazy dog
THE QUICK BROWN FOX JUMPS OVER THE LAZY DOG

TETRA B FAMILY

Tetra B Regular
Tetra B Bold

Norm
Zurich, Switzerland
1999

Tetra B, a monospaced font containing a number of special signs, was generated for a series of club flyers in Zurich.

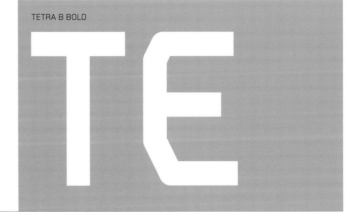

TETRA B BOLD

TONNAGE SANS

TONNAGE

ABCDEFGHIJKLMNO
PQRSTUVWXYZ
1234567890

TONNAGE SANS

THE QUICK BROWN FOX JUMPS OVER THE LAZY DOG

TONNAGE FAMILY

TONNAGE SANS
TONNAGE SERIF
TONNAGE MASK SANS
TONNAGE MASK SERIF

Miles Newlyn
x&y
London, UK
1996

Tonnage is a homage to David Harris's seminal Chromium typeface, which was influenced by his appreciation of toy, kitsch and vernacular objects.

TONNAGE SANS

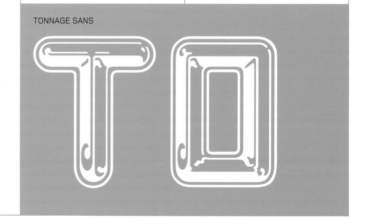

FOUNDRY ARCHITYPE VAN DOESBURG

UAN DOESBURG

ABBCDEFGHIJKLM
NOPQRSTUUWXYZ
1234567BB90

FOUNDRY ARCHITYPE VAN DOESBURG

THE QUICK BROWN FOX JUMPS OVER THE LAZY DOG
THE QUICK BROWN FOX JUMPS OVER THE LAZY DOG

FOUNDRY ARCHITYPE VAN DOESBURG FAMILY

UAN DOESBURG

David Quay/Freda Sack
The Foundry
London, UK
1996

Foundry Architype Van Doesburg is based on a 1919 alphabet by Theo van Doesburg which was formed from a square divided into twenty-five equal units.

FOUNDRY ARCHITYPE VAN DOESBURG

VMR

ABCDEFGHIJKLMNO
PQRSTUVWXYZ
1234567890

VMR

THE QUICK BROWN FOX JUMPS OVER THE LAZY DOG

VMR FAMILY

VMR

Julian Morey
Club Twenty-One
London, UK
1999

VMR was based on a typeface found in a London newsagent. The three letters of its name mean nothing, they were simply randomly selected from the alphabet.

VMR

WAR STEALTH PLANE

WAR STEALTH PLANE

The quick brown fox jumps over the lazy dog
THE QUICK BROWN FOX JUMPS OVER THE LAZY DOG

WAR FAMILY

WAR TORTURE
War Torture Flesh
War Torture Stitches
War Thermonuclear Bo
War Stealth Model
War Stealth Plane
WAR PANZER WW1
WAR FORWARD BOLD
War Explosion Part
War Explosion Total
War Commando
✕ ✕ ✕ ✕ ✕ ✕ ✕ ✕
⚡ ⚡ ⚡ ⚡ ⚡ ⚡ ⚡ ⚡
▦ ▦ ▦ ▦ ▦ ▦ ▦
╼◦╼╼◦╼╼◦╼╼◦╼╼◦╼╼◦╼

Tomi Haaparanta/Klaus
Haapaniemi/Brian Kaszonyi
Protokid
London, UK
1999/2000

War was designed to reflect both
the effects of war, and the
language of military technology.

WAR STEALTH PLANE

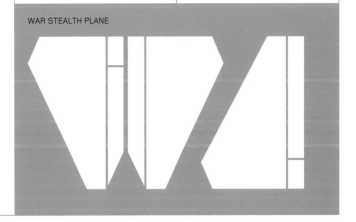

WORKING

WORKING

ABCDEFGHIJK LMNOPQRSTUV WXYZ

WORKING

THE QUICK BROWN FOX JUMPS OVER THE LAZY DOG

WORKING FAMILY

WORKING

Simon Gofton
Tom Hingston Studio
London, UK
2000

Working is one version of an experimental display font drawn for a Japanese music client. An amended, slightly more conventional version of the same font was used for the commercial campaign.

WORKING

ZERO CLOSED REGULAR

ZERO

AaBbCcDdEeFfGgHhIi
JjKkLlMmNnOoPpQqRr
SsTtUuVvWwXxYyZz
1234567890

ZERO CLOSED REGULAR

The quick brown fox jumps over the lazy dog
THE QUICK BROWN FOX JUMPS OVER THE LAZY DOG

ZERO FAMILY

Zero Closed Regular
Zero Open Regular

Nick Hayes
Identikal Foundry
London, UK
2000

Zero was originally produced for a
record label, and was based on the
pre-structured rhythms of music.

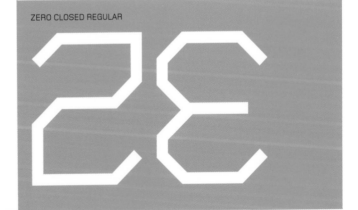

ZERO CLOSED REGULAR

DIET

DIET

AABBDCDDEEFFGGHHII
JJKKLLMMNNOOPPQQRR
SSTTUUUUWWXXYYZZ
1234567890

DIET

THE QUICK BROWN FOX JUMPS OVER THE LAZY DOG
THE QUICK BROWN FOX JUMPS OVER THE LAZY DOG

DIET FAMILY

DIET

Shin Sasaki
Extra Design
Sapporo, Japan
2001

Diet was designed specially
for TYPE 1 and is free on the CD
that accompanies this book. It is
an oblique, monoline version of
Threelines, also designed by Extra.

DIET

CIRCUMCISION CLASSIC 1.0

CIRCUMCISION

ᴅᴀᴇ§ᴄᴄᴏᴅᴈᴇᴇ∫ɢᴀʜıı

ʔıᴋᴋʟıᴍᴍɴᴀᴏᴅᴘᴅᴀʔʀ

§§ᴛᴛʊʊʊᴠᴅᴡᴡᴀᴀʏᴢᴢ

123ЧՏᏮ7ᏴᎺ0

CIRCUMCISION CLASSIC 1.0

the quick ϧroшᴀ ∫oᴀ ϳuᴘᴘᴈ oᴠᴇᴦ the lᴀzʏ ᴄᴏᴅ

THE QUICK BROШᴀ ∫OᴀϳUᴘᴘᴈOᴠᴇᴦTHE LᴀᏃʏOOᏮ

CIRCUMCISION FAMILY

CIRCUMCISION CLASSIC 1.0

CIRCUMCISION CLASSIC 1.1

CIRCUMCISION CLASSIC 2.0

CIRCUMCISION CLASSIC 2.1

Matius Gerardo Grieck
[+ism]
London, UK
1999

Circumcision is the result of the graphic deconstruction of the Hebrew script alphabet. One of the typeface's predominant visual characteristics is the reversed stroke ending, which is due to the right to left writing direction.

CIRCUMCISION CLASSIC 1.0

D.CAL

dcal

abcdefghijkl
mnopqrstuv
wxyz

D.CAL

the quick brown fox jumps over the lazy dog

D.CAL FAMILY

dcal

Ben Drury
London, UK
2000

D.cal is loosely inspired by
calligraphic bible script. It appears
to be rendered by a flat nib angled
at exactly 45°, but is in fact based
on two offset circles.

D.CAL

FF FANCY WRITING MEDIAN

FANCY WRITING

AaBbCcDdEeFfGgHhIiJjKk
LlMmNnOoPpQqRrSsTtUu
VvWwXxYyZz
1234567890

FF FANCY WRITING MEDIAN

the quick brown fox jumps over the lazy dog
THE QUICK BROWN FOX JUMPS OVER THE LAZY DOG

FF FANCY WRITING FAMILY

Fancy Writing Micro
Fancy Writing Median
Fancy Writing Mega

Timothy Donaldson
FSI FontShop International
Berlin, Germany
1996

FF Fancy Writing came from a desire to create handwritten letterforms in a digital manner. The letters were created using Painter, then autotraced.

FF FANCY WRITING MEDIAN

FF GRAFFIO DIFENSIVO

GRAFFIO

AaBbCcDdEeFfGgHhIi

JjKkLlMmNnOoPpQqRr

SsTtUuVvWwXxYyZz

1234567890

FF GRAFFIO DIFENSIVO

The quick brown fox jumps over the lazy dog
THE QUICK BROWN FOX JUMPS OVER THE LAZY DOG

FF GRAFFIO FAMILY

Graffio Difensivo
Graffio Offensivo

Alessio Leonardi
FSI FontShop International
Berlin, Germany
1995

FF Graffio is a nervous-looking typeface that was designed after a visit to the cinema to watch the film Natural Born Killers.

FF GRAFFIO DIFENSIVO

HALAAL

HALAAL

The quick brown fox jumps over the lazy dog
THE QUICK BROWN FOX JUMPS OVER THE LAZY DOG

HALAAL FAMILY

Sheila Dorje
Orange Juice Design
Cape Town, South Africa
2000

Halaal derives its inspiration from the act of facing what you think you know, to find that it is something very different. Upon looking a little more closely, you see that you can actually read what you may have thought was a different language.

HALAAL

INEXPRESSED

INEXPRESSED

abcdefgghijklmnopqr

qrstuvwxyz

1234567890

INEXPRESSED

THE quick brown fox jumps over the lazy dog
THE quick brown fox jumps over the lazy dog

INEXPRESSED FAMILY

INEXPRESSED

Claudio Piccinini
Thirstype
Barrington, US
1998

Inexpressed's twisting, repeating marks were created to reflect the anxiety and frustration of being unable to express what you want.

INEXPRESSED

INKDUP

iNKDUP

ABCDEFGHIJK
LMNOPQRSTU
VWXYZ

INKDUP

THE QUICK BROWN FOX JUMPS OVER THE LAZY DOG

INKDUP FAMILY

iNKDUP

Tyler Askew
Atlanta, US
2001

Inkdup is a gestural typeface
created with fingers and printing
inks. It was drawn backwards on
plexiglass, then printed face down
on to newsprint, scanned and
converted to outlines.

INKDUP

MW FAT

mW

AaBbCcDdEeFfGgHhIi
JjKkLlMmNnOoPpQqRr
SsTtUuVvWwXxYyZz
1234567891010

MW FAT

the quick brown fox jumps over the lazy dog
THE QUICK BROWN FOX JUMPS OVER THE LAZY DOG

MW FAMILY

mw Lite
mw Fat

Matt Wingfield
London, UK
2001

MW was designed in-house as part
of a large-scale graffiti window
display for Harvey Nichols
department store.

MW FAT

(NEW FORMULA) TIPPEX REGULAR

TIPPEX

@ABCÇDDEEFFGGHHII

JJKKLLMMNNOOPPQRR

SSTTUUVWWXXYYZZ

1234567890

(NEW FORMULA) TIPPEX REGULAR

THE QUICK BROWN FOX JUMPS OVER THE LAZY DOG
THE QUICK BROWN FOX JUMPS OVER THE LAZY DOG

(NEW FORMULA) TIPPEX FAMILY

TIPPEX REGULAR
Tippex Regular

Austin Cowdall
NEW
London, UK
2001

(NEW Formula) Tippex is part of a series of handmade fonts and, as its name suggests, was drawn using a bottle of Tippex.

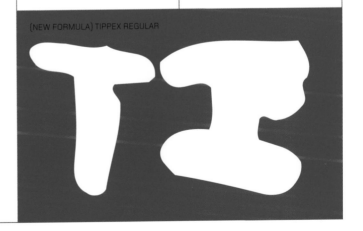

(NEW FORMULA) TIPPEX REGULAR

JOHNHADANIGHTMARE(LASTNIGHT)

JOHNHADANIGHTMARE

AaBbCcDdEeFfGgHhIiJj
KkLlMmNnOoPpQqRrSsTt
UuVvWwXxYyZz
1234567890

JOHNHADANIGHTMARE(LASTNIGHT)

The quick brown fox jumps over the lazy dog
THE QUICK BROWN FOX JUMPS OVER THE LAZY DOG

JOHNHADANIGHTMARE(LASTNIGHT) FAMILY

JohnHadANightmare

**Chester
Thirstype
Barrington, US
2001**

JohnHadANightmare(LastNight) was designed specially for TYPE 1 and is free on the CD that accompanies this book. The John in question could be Johannes Gutenberg, or just any John with taste and refinement.

JOHNHADANIGHTMARE(LASTNIGHT)

1ST AVENUE

1ST AVENUE

AaBbCcDdEeFfGgHhIi
JjKkLlMmNnOoPpQqRr
SsTtUuVvWwXxYyZz
1234567890

1ST AVENUE

The quick brown fox jumps over the lazy dog
THE QUICK BROWN FOX JUMPS OVER THE LAZY DOG

1ST AVENUE FAMILY

1st Avenue

Pablo Medina
Plazm Fonts
Portland, US
2000

1st Avenue was based on letters
from an old metal neon sign found
on First Avenue and Third Street,
New York. The inconsistencies were
achieved by cutting the digitized
letters apart and then pasting them
back together in Photoshop.

1ST AVENUE

FF AUTOTRACE DOUBLE

AUTOTRACE

AaBbCcDdEeFfGgHhIi
JjKkLlMmNnOoPpQqRr
SsTtUuVvWwXxYyZz
1234567890

FF AUTOTRACE DOUBLE

The quick brown fox jumps over the lazy dog
THE QUICK BROWN FOX JUMPS OVER THE LAZY DOG

FF AUTOTRACE FAMILY

Autotrace One
Autotrace Two
Autotrace Three
Autotrace Four
Autotrace Outline
Autotrace Six
Autotrace Seven
Autotrace Eight
Autotrace Nine
Autotrace Double

Neville Brody
FSI FontShop International
London, UK
1994

FF Autotrace is a series of sans serif typefaces combined and progressively distorted using the autotracing facility in Fontographer. Autotrace Double was created by superimposing Autotrace Two on top of Autotrace Nine.

FF AUTOTRACE DOUBLE

F CYBER STATIC

F CYBER STATIC

F CYBER STATIC FAMILY

Neville Brody
Fuse 14/FSI FontShop International
London, UK
1997

Cyber Static is built from randomly layered sequences of black and white halftone dots.

F CYBER STATIC

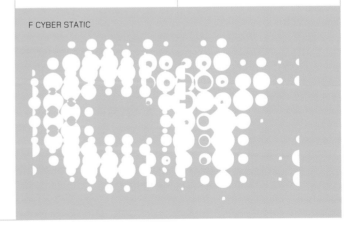

DEADGUN

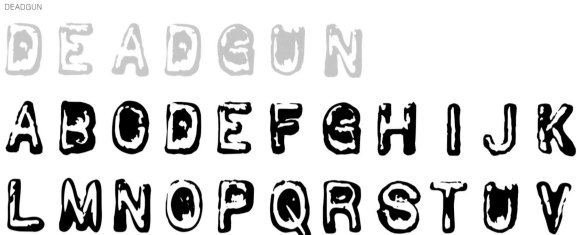

DEADGUN

THE QUICK BROWN FOX JUMPS OVER THE LAZY DOG

DEADGUN FAMILY

DEADGUN

Arjen Noordeman
The Chopping Block Inc.
New York, US
2000

Deadgun, which unmistakably references David Carson's unique graphic style, was created as a final tribute to his work on the cult magazine Raygun. It was conceived at Cranbrook Academy of Art in a workshop with Barry Deck.

DEADGUN

FF DIRTY FOUR

DIRTY

AaBbCcDdEeFfGgHhIi
JjKkLlMmNnOoPpQqRr
SsTtUuVvWwXxYyZz
1234567890

FF DIRTY FOUR

The quick brown fox jumps over the lazy dog
THE QUICK BROWN FOX JUMPS OVER THE LAZY DOG.

FF DIRTY FAMILY

Dirty One
Dirty One Bold
Dirty Three
Dirty Four
Dirty Six One
Dirty Seven One
Dirty Seven Two

Neville Brody
FSI FontShop International
London, UK
1994

FF Dirty is a reaction to the effortless clarity of digital typesetting. The family was originally designed for Dirty Faces, a collection of fonts published quarterly by FSI.

FF DIRTY FOUR

ITC DON'T PANIC

DON'T PANIC

ABBCCDDEEFGHIIJJKLLMMNN
OOPPQRRSTUUVWXXYZZ
1234567890

ITC DON'T PANIC

THE QUICK BROWN FOX JUMPS OVER THE LAZY DOG
THE QUICK BROWN FOX JUMPS OVER THE LAZY DOG

ITC DON'T PANIC FAMILY

PANIC
DON'T PANIC

Wayne Thompson
International Typeface Corporation
Wilmington, US
2000

ITC Don't Panic's inspiration came from type stamped on a ragged envelope received in the mail. The basic characters were laser printed, and then distressed, before being digitized and used as the basis for the rest of the design.

ITC DON'T PANIC

DOOM PLATOON MEDIUM

DOOM PLATOON

ABCDEFGHIJKLM
NOPQRSTUVWXYZ
1234567890

DOOM PLATOON MEDIUM

THE QUICK BROWN FOX JUMPS OVER THE LAZY DOG

DOOM PLATOON FAMILY

DOOM PLATOON MEDIUM
DOOM PLATOON BOLD

Rian Hughes
Device
London, UK
1996

Doom Platoon was developed from a logo design, also by Hughes, for DC Comics' Doom Patrol.

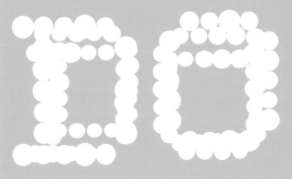

DOOM PLATOON MEDIUM

FAXSIMILE PLAIN

FAXSIMILE

AaBbCcDdEeFfGgHhIiJj
KkLlMmNnOoPpQqRrSs
TtUuVvWwXxYyZz
1234567890

FAXSIMILE PLAIN

The quick brown fox jumps over the lazy dog
THE QUICK BROWN FOX JUMPS OVER THE LAZY DOG

FAXSIMILE FAMILY

FAXSIMILE PLAIN
FAXSIMILE REVERSED

Andrew Smith
2Rebels
Quebec, Canada
1998

Faxsimile was constructed using a very old fax machine. Letters were enlarged on a photocopier to enhance the stressed effect, then each character was tweaked by hand leaving as much noise as possible.

FAXSIMILE PLAIN

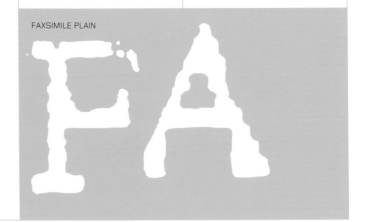

F FREEFORM TEXT

FREEFORM

AaBbCcDdEeFfGghIi
JjKkLlMmNnOoPpQqRr
SsTtUuVvWwXxYyZz
1234567890

F FREEFORM TEXT

The quick brown fox jumps over the lazy dog
THE QUICK BROWN FOX JUMPS OVER THE LAZY DOG

F FREEFORM FAMILY

Freeform Text
Composition

Neville Brody
Fuse 10/FSI FontShop International
London, UK
1996

F Freeform has five sets of abstract shapes and forms that are positioned on the keyboard according to intended relationships, creating endless possibilities of interactive combinations.

F FREEFORM TEXT

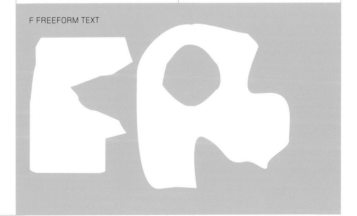

GUNSHOT

GUNSHOT

AABBCCDDEEFFGGHHIIJJ KKLLMMNNOOPPQQRRSSTT UUVVWWXXYYZZ 1234567890

GUNSHOT

THE QUICK BROWN FOX JUMPS OVER THE LAZY DOG
THE QUICK BROWN FOX JUMPS OVER THE LAZY DOG

GUNSHOT FAMILY

GUNSHOT

Swifty
Swifty Typografix
London, UK
1992

Gunshot was originally scanned and digitized from a road sign that had been shot with a shotgun, and was inspired by Sergio Leone movies. The uppercase character set has more holes than the lowercase set.

GUNSHOT

HAIRCUT SIR?

HAIRCUT SIR?

AABBCCDDEEFFGGHH II

JJKKLLMMNNOOPPQQRR

SSTTUUVVWWXXYYZZ

1234567890

HAIRCUT SIR?

THE QUICK BROWN FOX JUMPS OVER THE LAZY DOG
THE QUICK BROWN FOX JUMPS OVER THE LAZY DOG

HAIRCUT SIR? FAMILY

HAIRCUT SIR?

Lee Basford
Fluid
Birmingham, UK
1999

Haircut Sir? originates from an old press-in letter price board found in the attic of a hairdresser. The individual characters were scanned and then redrawn with deliberately random kerning and spacing for a more analogue appearance.

HAIRCUT SIR?

LINI VIER

LINI

ABCDEFGHIJK
LMNOPQRSTUI
WXYZ

LINI VIER

THE QUICK BROWN FOX JUMPS OIER THE LAZY DOG

LINI FAMILY

LINI DREI

LINI IIER

LINI IIER EO

Achim Reichert
Vier5
forhomeorofficeuse.com
Frankfurt, Germany
2000

Lini was intended to be bold and straight, but not technical. The idea came from working on an artist's catalogue containing objects and collages that formed loops.

LINI VIER

MANSIONS

MANSIONS

ÄABCCDGEPFⱻ⌐XHIJJKCLL

Mₐᴦ⌐⌐ObP₂⌐ᴦⅠS⌐

Tⴸⴸⵉ⌐ⵉⴸⵈⴸⵈⵈⵉ⌐Ⴤ2⌐

1234Jⴸⴸⵎ⌐4□

MANSIONS

THE ꟼⴸⵉ ꟼⴸꟼⵎ Fⴸⴸ ꟼⴸ⌐ⵉⵎⵎ OⴸⴸEꟼ FⵈE Lⴸℤⵉ □ꟼⵎ
THE QⴸⴸICK GROⴸⴸⵎ FOX Jⴸⴸⴸꟼⵎ OⴸVER THE Lⴸℤⵉ JOⴸ⌐

MANSIONS FAMILY

Mₐⴸ⌐ⵉⴸⵈⵎ⌐ⵎ

Florian Heiss
Scheufler & Heiss
London, UK
2001

Mansions is a semi-unreadable
pattern maker that's good used
with minus leading and kerning. The
forms derive from an 18th-century
woodcut type that has been filtered
through Photoshop until nothing of
the original remains.

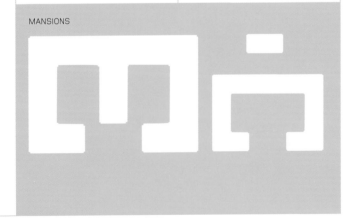

MANSIONS

BD PLAKATBAU

PLAKATBAU

AaBbCcDdEeFfGgHhIi
JjKkLlMmNnOoPpQqRr
SsTtUuVvWwXxYyZz
1234567890

BD PLAKATBAU

The quick brown fox jumps over the lazy dog
THE QUICK BROWN FOX JUMPS OVER THE LAZY DOG

BD PLAKATBAU FAMILY

Plakatbau

Lopetz
Büro Destruct
Bern, Switzerland
1995

BD Plakatbau, used on the cover of Radiohead albums Kid A and Amnesiac, was influenced by the Bauhaus typeface designs of Herbert Bayer.

BD PLAKATBAU

POSITIVE IDENT

POSITIVE IDENT

AaBbCcDdEeFfGgHhIi
JjKkLlMmNnOoPpQqRr
SsTtUuVvWwXxYyZz
1234567890

POSITIVE IDENT

The quick brown fox jumps over the lazy dog
THE QUICK BROWN FOX JUMPS OVER THE LAZY DOG

POSITIVE IDENT FAMILY

Positive Ident

Swifty
Swifty Typografix
London, UK
1996

Positive Ident is a hand-drawn eclectic font inspired by old sci-fi movie posters.

POSITIVE IDENT

PROCESS

A B C D E F G H I J K L M N O
P Q R S T U V W X Y Z
1 2 3 4 5 6 7 8 9 0

PROCESS

THE QUICK BROWN FOX JUMPS OVER THE LAZY DOG

PROCESS FAMILY

PROCESS

Lee Fasciani
Intro
London, UK
1997

Process was created by expanding on the effect achieved by the mechanical printing of a 'best before' date on a cardboard carton.

PROCESS

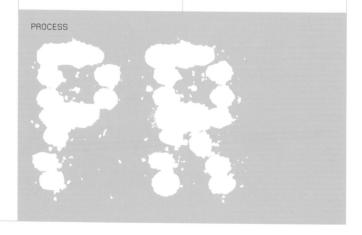

PTONAR

ptonar

abcdefghijklmn

opqrstuvwxyz

PTONAR

the quick brown fox jumps over the lazy dog

PTONAR FAMILY

ptonar

John Randle
London, UK
1996

PTonar was created using a very old inkjet printer with a broken nozzle. The experiment was to use only digital equipment to deconstruct and destroy typefaces and then to reconstruct them into different character forms.

PTONAR

RELEASE

ᴿᴱᴸᴱᴬˢᴱ

Aa Bb Cc Dd Ee Ff Gg Hh Ii
Jj Kk Ll Mm Nn Oo Pp Qq Rr
Ss Tt Uu Vv Ww Xx Yy Zz
1234567890

RELEASE

The quick brown fox jumps over the lazy dog
THE QUICK BROWN FOX JUMPS OVER THE LAZY DOG

RELEASE FAMILY

Release

Jeremy Dean
House Industries
Delaware, US
1989

Release comes from a collection of fonts named Flyer Fonts, all of which were created using a photocopier, various stencil kits and acrylic ink. Its inspiration was drawn from a logotype on a flyer for the punk band Pressure Release.

RELEASE

RHEOSTAT FAHRENHEIT BOOK

RHEOSTAT

AaBbCcDdEeFfGgHhIiJj

KkLlMmNnOoPpQqRrSs

TtUuVvWwXxYyZz

1234567890

RHEOSTAT FAHRENHEIT BOOK

The quick brown fox jumps over the lazy dog
THE QUICK BROWN FOX JUMPS OVER THE LAZY DOG·

RHEOSTAT FAMILY

Rheostat Celsius Lite
Rheostat Celsius Book
Rheostat Celsius Medium
Rheostat Celsius Bold
Rheostat Fahrenheit Lite
Rheostat Fahrenheit Book
Rheostat Fahrenheit Book Italic
Rheostat Fahrenheit Medium
Rheostat Fahrenheit Bold

Chester
Thirstype
Barrington, US
1996

Rheostat is based on a dot matrix grid of circles that vary in size in an approximation of brush lettering. The shape of the letterforms was also inspired by Barry Deck's Template Gothic.

RHEOSTAT FAHRENHEIT BOOK

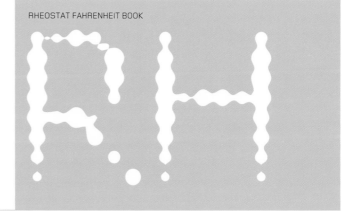

SHOEREPAIRS KNOCKOUT

SHOEREPAIRS

AaBbCcDdEeFfGgHhIi
JjKkLlMmNnOoPpQqRr
SsTtUuVvWwXxYyZz
1234567890

SHOEREPAIRS KNOCKOUT

The quick brown fox jumps over the lazy dog
THE QUICK BROWN FOX JUMPS OVER THE LAZY DOG

SHOEREPAIRS FAMILY

ShoeRepairs Regular
ShoeRepairs Italic
ShoeRepairs Knockout
ShoeRepairs Outline
ShoeRepairs Shadow
ShoeRepairs Display

Brode Vosloo
T-26 Digital Type Foundry
Durban, South Africa
2000

ShoeRepairs was born out of the need for an authentic African font, and clearly references the naïvety and originality of traditional hand-painted signage. Its six variations are designed to work together interchangeably.

SHOEREPAIRS KNOCKOUT

SLICE OF CAKE

SLICE OF CAKE

A ĄABBÇCĊDDĘÈÊFFGĞHHĮĪĨJJKKĻĻMMNŅ
OÖPPQQRŘSŠTŤUUVVVWWXXYŸŽŻ
1234567890

SLICE OF CAKE

THE QUICK BROWN FOX JUMPS OVER THE LAZY DOG
THE QUICK BROWN FOX JUMPS OVER THE LAZY DOG

SLICE OF CAKE FAMILY

SLICE OF CAKE

Swifty
Swifty Typografix
London, UK
1996

Slice of Cake was scanned and digitized from plastic cake decorations. The inspiration for the font came via Airfix model-making kits. The dash keys and left and right arrows are used to add the bars above or below the letters.

SLICE OF CAKE

F SURVEILLANCE VICTIMS

[decorative display type: SURVEILLANCE]

[decorative display alphabet: A B C D E F G H I J K L M N O P Q R S T U V W X Y Z]

[decorative numerals: 1234567890]

F SURVEILLANCE VICTIMS

[decorative display type: THE QUICK BROWN FOX JUMPS OVER THE LAZY DOG]

F SURVEILLANCE FAMILY

[decorative display type: SURVEILLANCE VICTIMS]

[pictogram/dingbat glyphs: surveillance scenes and silhouettes]

Florian Heiss
Scheufler & Heiss
Fuse 17/ FSI FontShop International
London, UK
1997

F Surveillance has a family of four styles which allows the user either to change perspective on crime scenes, or to create crime scenes showing the date and time.

F SURVEILLANCE VICTIMS

U.S.EH

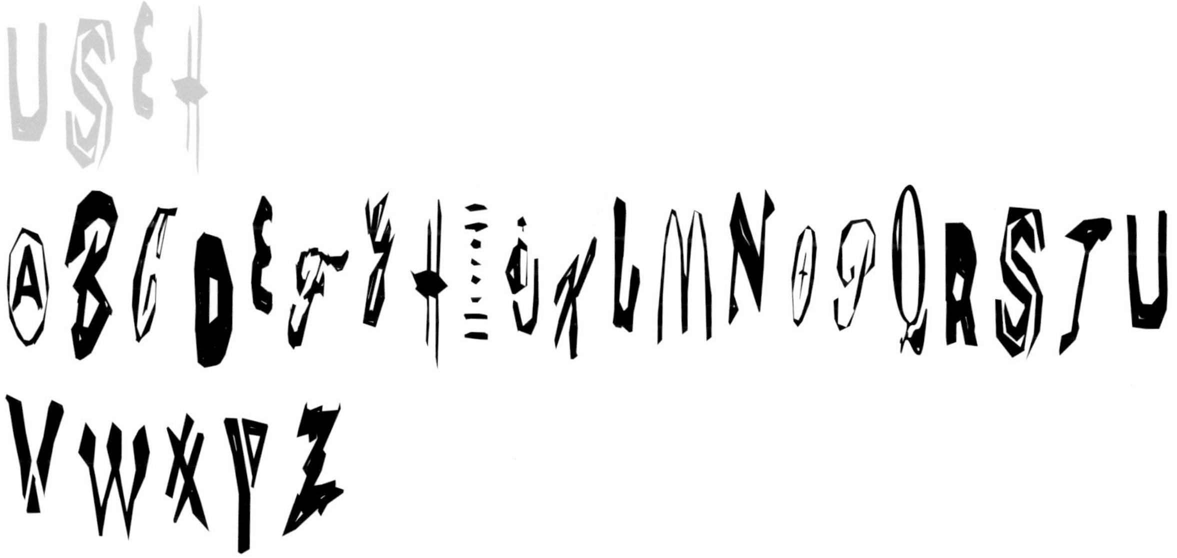

USE+

@BCDEFYHIKLMNOPQRSTU
VWXYZ

U.S.EH

THE QUICK BROWN FOX JUMPS OVER THE LAZY DOG

U.S.EH FAMILY

USE+

Paul Sych
Thirstype
Barrington, US
1994

U.S.Eh is made from the processed logotypes of American corporate companies such as Ford, Kellogg's and McDonald's.

U.S.EH

US

ASPHALT

ASPHALT

ABCDEFGHIJKLMNOPQRSTUVWXYZ

1234567890

ASPHALT

THE QUICK BROWN FOX JUMPS OVER THE LAZY DOG

ASPHALT FAMILY

ASPHALT

Masahiko Nakamura
Lineto
Zurich, Switzerland
2001

Asphalt was designed specially
for TYPE 1 and is free on the CD
that accompanies this book. It was
sampled from photographs taken of
European road markings.

ASPHALT

AXIS OUTLINE

ABCDEFGHIJKLMNOP
QRSTUVWXYZ
1234567890

AXIS OUTLINE

THE QUICK BROWN FOX JUMPS OVER THE LAZY DOG

AXIS FAMILY

AXIS
AXIS OUTLINE

Julian Morey
Club Twenty-One
London, UK
2001

Axis Outline is a typeface based on
plastic stencil lettering.

AXIS OUTLINE

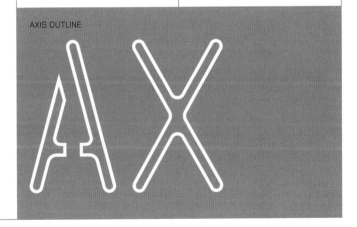

BAD EGGS

BAD EGGS

AaBbCcDdEeFFGgHhIiJj
KkLIMmNnOoPpQqRr
SsTtUuVvWwXxYyZz
1234567890

BAD EGGS

The quick brown fox jumps over the lazy dog
THE QUICK BROWN FOX JUMPS OVER THE LAZY DOG

BAD EGGS FAMILY

Bad Eggs

Swifty
Swifty Typografix
London, UK
1997

Bad Eggs is a hand-drawn stencil font that works well at both large and small sizes. Additional interlocking characters are currently in development.

BAD EGGS

BRONXVILLE

BRONXVILLE

ABCDEFGHIJKLMNOP
QRSTTUVWXXYZZ
1234567890

BRONXVILLE

THE QUICK BROWN FOX JUMPS OVER THE LAZY DOG
THE QUICK BROWN FOX JUMPS OVER THE LAZY DOG

BRONXVILLE FAMILY

BRONXVILLE
BRONXVILLE MONO

Julian Morey
Club Twenty-One
London, UK
2001

Bronxville has a hard, geometric stress and unusually fine breaks between stencil shapes. A true monospaced version of the font is also available, perfect for stacking letters.

BRONXVILLE

FF CHERNOBYL

CHERNOBYL

AaBbCcDdEeFFGgHhIiJjKk
LlMmNnOoPpQqRrSsTtUu
VvWwXxYyZz
1234567890

FF CHERNOBYL

The quick brown fox jumps over the lazy dog
THE QUICK BROWN FOX JUMPS OVER THE LAZY DOG

FF CHERNOBYL FAMILY

Chernobyl

Stephan Mueller
Lineto
FSI FontShop International
Zurich, Switzerland
1998

FF Chernobyl was based on a newspaper clipping of the Chernobyl nuclear power station disaster. A picture of one of the reactor buildings showed huge stencilled letters, from which a complete character set was drawn.

FF CHERNOBYL

COMSAT BOX

COMSAT

AaBbCcDdEeFfGgHhIi JjKkLlMmNnOoPpQqRr SsTtUuJuWwXxYyZz 1234567890

COMSAT BOX

The quick brown fox jumps over the lazy dog
THE QUICK BROWN FOX JUMPS OVER THE LAZY DOG

COMSAT FAMILY

Comsat Stealth
Comsat Unit
Comsat Box
Comsat Box Italic
Comsat Station
Comsat Fat
Comsat Storm

Malte Haust
Bionic Systems
T–26 Digital Type Foundry
Düsseldorf, Germany
1998

Comsat, an abbreviation of communications satellite, combines the matrix fonts of the US Navy's communication systems with the stencil type which appears on the wings of their aircraft.

COMSAT BOX

CUT IT OUT

CUT IT OUT

AaBbCcDdEeFfGgHhIiJjKkLlMmNn OoPpQqRrSsTtUuVvWwXxYyZz 1234567890

CUT IT OUT

The quick brown fox jumps over the lazy dog
THE QUICK BROWN FOX JUMPS OVER THE LAZY DOG

CUT IT OUT FAMILY

Cut It Out

Swifty
Swifty Typografix
London, UK
1995

Cut It Out is an organic stencil font designed for use at a large scale. It was drawn using straight lines, cut out of card as a stencil, sprayed, scanned, outlined and then digitized.

CUT IT OUT

DESIGNATE

DESIGNATE

AaBbCcDdEeFfGgHhIi
JjKkLlMmNnOoPpQq
RrSsTtUuVvWwXxYyZz
1234567890

DESIGNATE

The quick brown fox jumps over the lazy dog
THE QUICK BROWN FOX JUMPS OVER THE LAZY DOG

DESIGNATE FAMILY

Designate

Hideki Inaba
Hideki Inaba Design
Tokyo, Japan
1999

Designate, used in +81 magazine
(also designed by Inaba), was based
on rubber stamp typefaces.

DESIGNATE

FAT ARSE

FAT ARSE

AaBbCc2dEeFfGg

HhIiJjKkLlMmNn

OoPpQqRrSsTtUu

UuWwXxYyZz

1234567890

FAT ARSE

The quick brown fox jumps over the lazy dog
THE QUICK BROWN FOX JUMPS OVER THE LAZY DOG

FAT ARSE FAMILY

Fat Arse

Mitch
London, UK
1997

Fat Arse is based on the shapes made by the plan view of a 1970s leather sofa. You can clearly see this sofa shape in the letter A, the first character to be designed. The font was first used in print in Straight No Chaser magazine.

FAT ARSE

FUCKING GOOD STENCIL

FG STENCIL

**ABCDEFGHIJKLM
NOPQRSTUVWXYZ
1234567890**

FUCKING GOOD STENCIL

THE QUICK BROWN FOX JUMPS OVER THE LAZY DOG

FUCKING GOOD STENCIL FAMILY

FG STENCIL

Jonathan Hitchen
Beaufonts
Manchester, UK
1996

Fucking Good Stencil is a reaction to designers' tendencies to over-justify and over-analyse what are essentially decorative design ideas.

FUCKING GOOD STENCIL

JAKARTA

JAKARTA

ABCCDEFGHIJKLMM
NOPQRSTUVWXYZ
1234567890

JAKARTA

THE QUICK BROWN FOX JUMPS OVER THE LAZY DOG
THE QUICK BROWN FOX JUMPS OVER THE LAZY DOG

JAKARTA FAMILY

JAKARTA

Julian Morey
Club Twenty-One
London, UK
2000

Jakarta is based on a combination
of stencil type and 1950s American
high school sweatshirts.

JAKARTA

PERPETUAL

PERPETUAL

AaBbCcDdEeFfGgHhi
JjKkLlMmNnOoPpQqRr
SsTtUuVvWwXxYyZz
1234567890

PERPETUAL

The quick brown fox jumps over the lazy dog
THE QUICK BROWN FOX JUMPS OVER THE LAZY DOG

PERPETUAL FAMILY

Perpetual

Mitch
London, UK
1998

Perpetual was originally based on a single continuous line, hence the name, but was further developed until only a few characters adhered to this original concept. It was created for the electronic band Red Snapper.

PERPETUAL

ROADWORKS

ROADWORKS

ABCDEFGHIJKLMNOP
QRSTUVWXYZ
1234567890

ROADWORKS

THE QUICK BROWN FOX JUMPS OVER THE LAZY DOG

ROADWORKS FAMILY

ROADWORKS
PAINTWORKS

Julian Morey
Club Twenty-One
London, UK
1992

Roadworks was produced with a limited budget as a raw and basic identity for a record label and nightclub. When redigitizing the typeface, Paintworks was the result of using the autotrace.

ROADWORKS

RO

ARS TEGEL

TEGEL

AaBbCcDdEeFfGgHhIi
JjKkLlMmNnOoPpQqRr
SsTtUuVvWwXxYyZz
1234567890

ARS TEGEL

The quick brown fox jumps over the lazy dog
THE QUICK BROWN FOX JUMPS OVER THE LAZY DOG

ARS TEGEL FAMILY

Tegel
Tegel Alternate
Tegel Small Caps

Angus R. Shamal
ARS Type
Amsterdam, The Netherlands
1998

ARS Tegel experiments with the limitation of grid systems. The objective was to create a complete operational display character set from a 3 x 5 grid.

ARS TEGEL

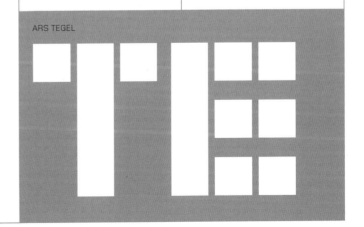

UNKLE

UNKLE

A B C D E F G H I J K

L M N O P Q R S T U

V W X Y Z

UNKLE

THE QUICK BROWN FOX JUMPS OVER THE LAZY DOG

UNKLE FAMILY

UNKLE

Ben Drury
London, UK
1998

Unkle was originally based on the type used in the 1980 Disney film Tron. It was designed specifically for the Unkle recording project and was used on the album Psyence Fiction.

UNKLE

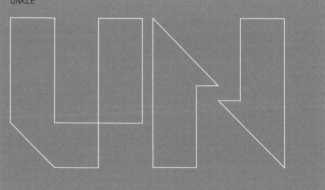

FF WATER TOWER

WATER TOWER

AaBbCcDdEeFfGgHhIi
JjKkLlMmNnOoPpQqRr
SsTtUuVvWwXxYyZz
1234567890

FF WATER TOWER

The quick brown fox jumps over the lazy dog
THE QUICK BROWN FOX JUMPS OVER THE LAZY DOG

FF WATER TOWER FAMILY

Water Tower
WATER TOWER CAPS

Cornel Windlin
Lineto
FSI FontShop International
Zurich, Switzerland
1998

FF Water Tower was initially drawn for the cover of a book on Rachel Whiteread's Water Tower art project in New York. It was inspired by the stencilled characters found on the city's fire doors, emergency exits and taxi cabs.

FF WATER TOWER

CIRCUIT

CIRCUIT

AABBCCDDEEFFGGHH
IIJJKKLLMMNNOPPQ
RRSSTTUVVWWXXYYZZ
1234567890

CIRCUIT

THE QUICK BROWN FOX JUMPS OVER THE LAZY DOG
THE QUICK BROWN FOX JUMPS OVER THE LAZY DOG

CIRCUIT FAMILY

CIRCUIT

David Rust
Optimo
Lausanne, Switzerland
2001

Circuit was designed specially for TYPE 1 and is free on the CD that accompanies this book. Its design was inspired by plastic letters used in a local garage.

CIRCUIT

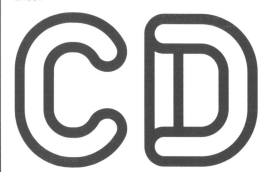

AGIP

AGIP

AaBbCcDdEeFfGgHhIi JjKkLIMmNnOoPpQqRr SsTtUuVvWwXxYyZz 1234567890

AGIP

The quick brown fox jumps over the lazy dog
THE QUICK BROWN FOX JUMPS OVER THE LAZY DOG

AGIP FAMILY

Agip

Laurence Jaccottet/
Niels Wehrspann
//copy//
Lausanne, Switzerland
2001

Agip is based on the logotype of AgipPetroli, producers of engine fuels and lubricants. It was digitized for the book Benzin: Junge Schweitzer Graphik, 'Benzin' meaning fuel in German.

AGIP

AUT FRAT

AUT FRAT
ABCDEFGHIJKLMN
OPQRSTUVWXYZ
1234567890

AUT FRAT

THE QUICK BROWN FOX JUMPS OVER THE LAZY DOG

AUT FRAT FAMILY

AUT FRAT

Tim Fletcher
Typical
London, UK
2000

Aut Frat was designed specifically for the book 100% Cotton: T-shirt Graphics. It is a modern interpretation of the classic American college typeface.

AUT FRAT

JAKITA WIDE INLINE

JAKITA

AaBbCcDdEeFfGg
HhIiJjKkLlMmNnOo
PpQqRrSsTtUuVv
WwXxYyZz
1234567890

JAKITA WIDE INLINE

The quick brown fox jumps over the lazy dog
THE QUICK BROWN FOX JUMPS OVER THE LAZY DOG

JAKITA FAMILY

Jakita Wide
Jakita Wide Bold
Jakita Wide Inline

Rian Hughes
Device
London, UK
2000

Jakita was developed for the Transient Records' dancemusic.com corporate identity. It was designed to lend itself to web rasteration, but also works well in print.

JAKITA WIDE INLINE

AF ONELINE

ONELINE

AaBbCcDdEeFfGgHhIiJjKk

LlMmNnOoPpQqRrSsTtUu

VvWwXxYyZz

1234567890

AF ONELINE

The quick brown fox jumps over the lazy dog
THE QUICK BROWN FOX JUMPS OVER THE LAZY DOG

AF ONELINE FAMILY

Oneline

Anne Wehebrink
Acme Fonts
London, UK
1998

AF Oneline was produced using a system which allowed its form to be determined by an initial set of design principles. The result is an outline version of the font AF Carplates, designed by Sandy Suffield and Christian Küsters.

AF ONELINE

PARALINE

PARALINE

PARALINE

THE QUICK BROWN FOX JUMPS OVER THE LAZY DOG
THE QUICK BROWN FOX JUMPS OVER THE LAZY DOG

PARALINE FAMILY

Paraline

Shin Sasaki
Extra Design
Sapporo, Japan
2001

Paraline was created using circles, right angles and parallel lines, with the thickness of the lines and the space between the lines always remaining equal.

PARALINE

PICO WHITE

Pico

abcdeFghjkImmno
PpQqrstuvwxYyz
1234567890

PICO WHITE

the quick brown fox jumps over the lazy dog
the Quick brown Fox jumps over the lazy dog

PICO FAMILY

Pico black
Pico white

Masayuki Sato
Maniackers Design
Takasaki, Japan
2001

Pico was designed to be a cute typeface that could also be used as a logotype.

PICO WHITE

PUNCH R4

PUNCH

AaBbCcDdEeFfGgHhIiJj
KkLlMmNnOoPpQqRrSs
TtUuVvWwXxYyZz
1234567890

PUNCH R4

The quick brown fox jumps over the lazy dog
THE QUICK BROWN FOX JUMPS OVER THE LAZY DOG

PUNCH FAMILY

Punch R1
Punch R2
Punch R3
Punch R4
Punch S1
Punch S2
Punch S3
Punch S4

Rick Valicenti/Gregg Brokaw
Thirstype
Barrington, US
1998

Punch was co-created by a designer for use in print and by an animator for use in animation.

PUNCH R4

THREELINES

THREELINES

AABBCCDDEEFFGGHHII
JJKKLLMMNOOPPQQRR
SSTTUUVVWWXXYYZZ
1234567890

THREELINES

THE QUICK BROWN FOX JUMPS OVER THE LAZY DOG
THE QUICK BROWN FOX JUMPS OVER THE LAZY DOG

THREELINES FAMILY

THREELINES

Shin Sasaki
Extra Design
Sapporo, Japan
2001

Threelines initially consisted of only five characters, and was drawn specifically as a logotype for Extra Design in 2000.

THREELINES

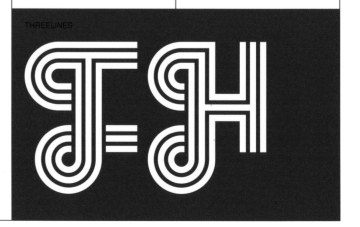

WYTRI

wytri

abcdefghijklmno

pqrstuvwxyz

1234567890

WYTRI

the quick brown fox jumps over the lazy dog

WYTRI FAMILY

wytri

Tim Fletcher
Typical
London, UK
2001

Wytri was developed for a
multimedia exhibition space and bar
in London called Wire. The overall
structure came from the idea of
live, neutral and earth wires found in
household plugs and sockets.

WYTRI

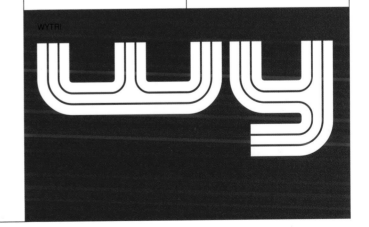

STUDIO

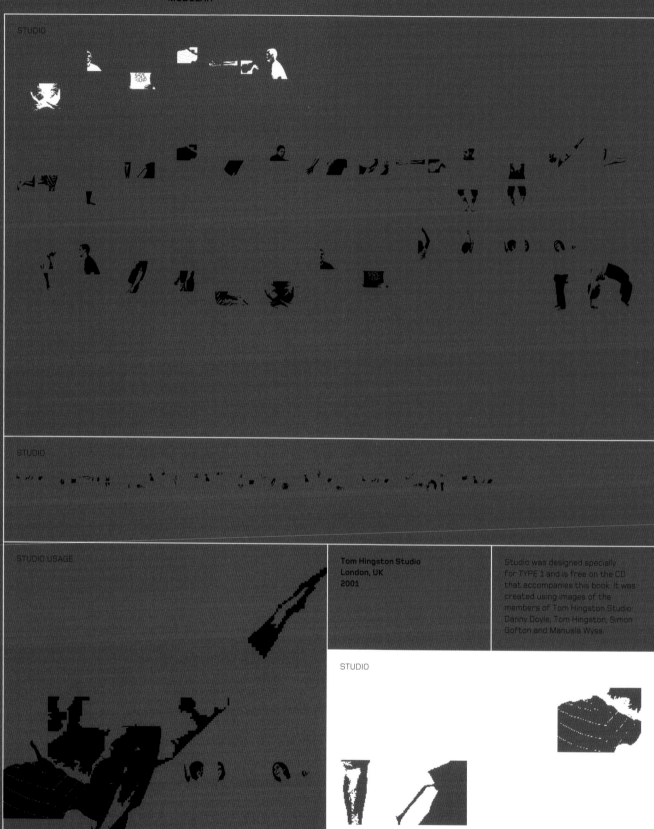

STUDIO

STUDIO USAGE

Tom Hingston Studio
London, UK
2001

Studio was designed specially
for TYPE 1 and is free on the CD
that accompanies this book. It was
created using images of the
members of Tom Hingston Studio:
Danny Doyle, Tom Hingston, Simon
Gofton and Manuela Wyss.

STUDIO

FY BAUHAUS

BAUHAUS

AaBbCcDdEeFfGgHhIiJj

KkLlMmNnOoPpQqRrSsTt

UuVvWwXxYyZz

1234567890

FY BAUHAUS

The quick brown fox jumps over the lazy dog
THE QUICK BROWN FOX JUMPS OVER THE LAZY DOG

FY BAUHAUS FAMILY

Bauhaus

Henrik Kubel/Scott Williams
A2-Graphics/SW/HK
fontyoufonts.com
London, UK
2001

FY Bauhaus was strongly inspired by
a typeface developed in 1925 by
Josef Albers.

FY BAUHAUS

BECKER LIGHT

BECKER

AABC<DD EEF FGGHI
JJ KKL IMMNOP POQRR
SSI+UIIVV UWXYYZZ
1234567890

BECKER LIGHT

THE QUI<K BROWN FOX JUMPS OV ER +HE IAZY DOG
THE QUICK BROWN FOX JUMPS OVER THE LAZY DOG

BECKER FAMILY

BE<KER LIGH+
BE<KER LIGH+ I+AII<
BE<KER BOID

Miles Newlyn
x&y
London, UK
1997

Becker is a carefully balanced monospaced matrix that provides changes in weight and slant. Now in common use on electrical appliances throughout the home, its legibility goes unquestioned.

BECKER LIGHT

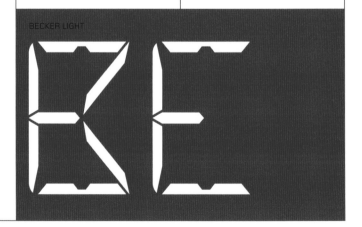

BELT 9

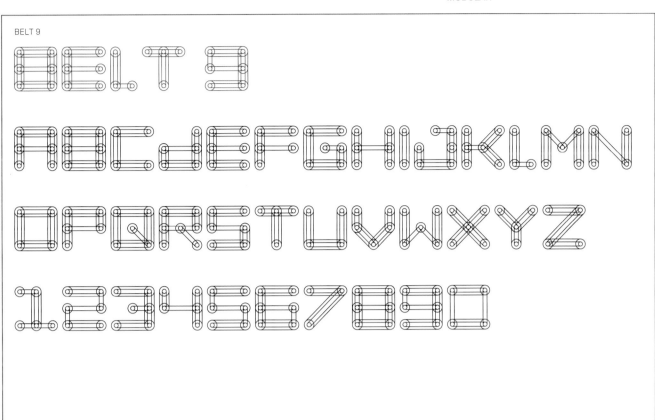

BELT 9

THE QUICK BROWN FOX JUMPS OVER THE LAZY DOG

BELT 9 FAMILY

BELT 9

Mike Kohnke
We Associated
Oakland, US
1999

Belt 9 was inspired by
architectural concepts and
analytical diagrams. Each letter
was rendered from a base of nine
circles. A series of belts link the
circles or pulleys to create these
mechanical-looking letterforms.

BELT 9

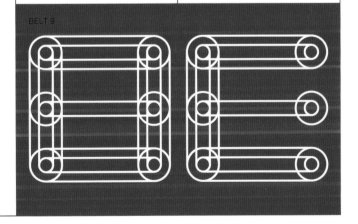

CHECKOUT REGULAR

CHECKOUT

AaBbCcDdEeFfGgHhIi
JJKkL1MmNnOoPpQqRr
SsTtUuVvWwXxYyZz
1234567890

CHECKOUT REGULAR

The quick brown fox jumps over the lazy dog
THE QUICK BROWN FOX JUMPS OVER THE LAZY DOG

CHECKOUT FAMILY

Checkout Extra Light
Checkout Light
Checkout Regular
Checkout Bold
Checkout Black

Julian Morey
Club Twenty-One
London, UK
1998

Checkout is a dot matrix typeface based on supermarket till receipts. It has also been produced in condensed and extended versions, each in three weights.

CHECKOUT REGULAR

HALF-BAKED, HALF-UNCIAL

CHINESE WHISPERS

AaBbCcDdEeFfGgHhIiJj

KkLlMmNnOoPpQqRrSsTt

UuXxVvWwXxYyZz

1234567890

HALF-BAKED, HALF-UNCIAL

The quick brown fox jumps over the lazy dog
THE QUICK BROWN FOX JUMPS OVER THE LAZY DOG

CHINESE WHISPERS FAMILY

Aino
Fluid Woodbloc♥
Half-baked, half-uncial
Mental ist stencilist
Woodtype From
Outerspace

Ian Mitchell
Beaufonts
Liverpool, UK
2000/2001

Chinese Whispers is a type family designed by participants in an online project which invited people around the world to respond to letterforms created by Yaki Molcho, David Crow, Tobias Frere-Jones, Jonathan Hitchen and Erik van Blokland.

HALF-BAKED, HALF-UNCIAL

CRATER

crater

ABCDEFGHIJ
HLMNOPQRSTU
UWXYZ
1234567890

CRATER

THE QUICK BROWN FOX JUMPS OVER THE LAZY DOG
THE QUICK BROWN FOX JUMPS OVER THE LAZY DOG

CRATER FAMILY

crater

Nathan Gale
Brighton, UK
2001

Crater was designed specially for
TYPE 1 and is free on the CD that
accompanies this book. It was
inspired by a combination of
the plotting points on space
photography and a block of flats in
South London.

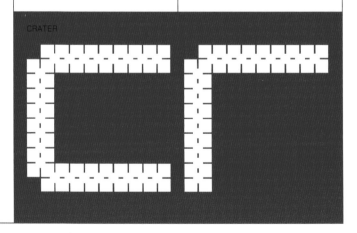

CRATER

CR TECHNO

cr techno

ABCDEFGHIJK
LMNOPQRSTUV
WXYZ
1234567890

CR TECHNO

THE QUICK BROWN FOX JUMPS OVER THE LAZY DOG

CR TECHNO FAMILY

cr techno

Nathan Gale
Brighton, UK
1998

CR Techno was designed for use within Creative Review magazine. It is a square monospaced typeface, made from a square matrix for a square format magazine.

CR TECHNO

EUROCHIP

EUROCHIP

EUROCHIP

The quick brown fox jumps over the lazy dog
THE QUICK BROWN FOX JUMPS OVER THE LAZY DOG

EUROCHIP FAMILY

Eurochip

Gilles Gavillet
Optimo
Lausanne, Switzerland
1998

Eurochip is constructed from the grid of a standard European electronic chip.

EUROCHIP

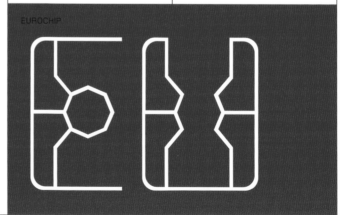

ARS FORTUNE

FORLUNE

AƏBbCDDeFrG9HHI ι JJ

KkLLMNnOoPPDPRrSƏt

UυᐯᵂXxYy22

1234SG7890

ARS FORTUNE

the qui Ck bro4n Fox JuMPs over the Lazy do9

tHE QUI CK BRO4N FOX JUMPS OVER tHE LAZY DOG

ARS FORTUNE FAMILY

Fortunr

Angus R. Shamal
ARS Type
Amsterdam, The Netherlands
2000

ARS Fortune evolved from sketches and ideas recalling the limitations and charms of electric letter signage. Its design was inspired by the notion that commerce and fortune are the foundations of modern society.

ARS FORTUNE

HIVE BASE

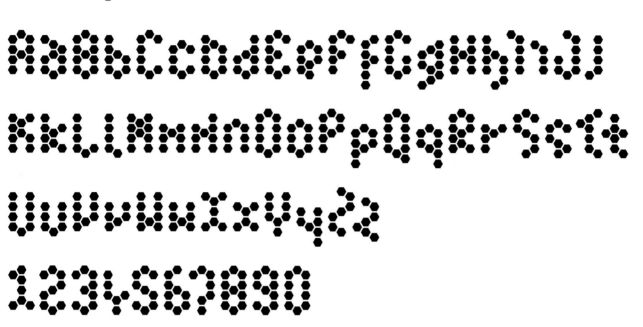

HIVE BASE

The quick brown fox jumps over the lazy dog
THE QUICK BROWN FOX JUMPS OVER THE LAZY DOG

HIVE FAMILY

Hive Base

Hive Drone

Hive Unit

Jakob Straub
T–26 Digital Type Foundry
Berlin, Germany
2000

Hive was inspired by beehives, and in contrast to dot matrix fonts based on more rigid templates, the hexagonal grid creates a playful floating baseline.

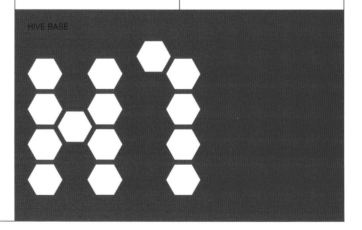

HIVE BASE

LEGO PM/AM

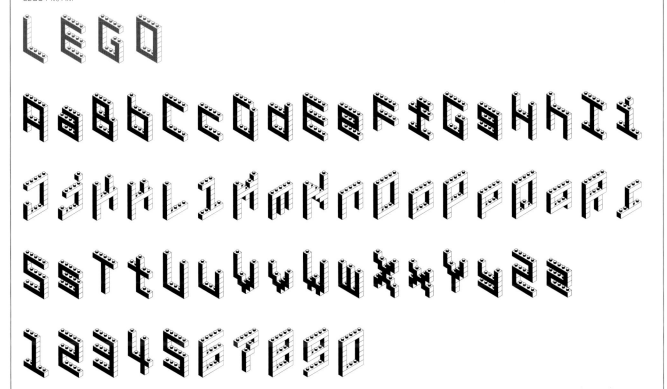

LEGO PM/AM

The quick brown fox jumps over the lazy dog
THE QUICK BROWN FOX JUMPS OVER THE LAZY DOG

LEGO FAMILY

Lego PM
Lego AM

Urs Lehni
Lineto
Zurich, Switzerland
1999

Lego has been developed both as a typeface, and also as a small design application which allows users to build letters, images or even whole environments using a library of pre-set elements.

LEGO PM

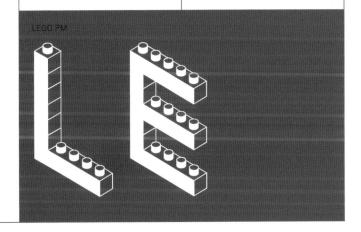

LIQUID CRYSTAL

LIQUID CRYSTAL

AaBBCDDEEFGHII
JJKLMMNOPQRRS
TTUVWWXYYZ
1234567890

LIQUID CRYSTAL

THE QUICK BROWN FOX JUMPS OVER THE LAZY DOG
THE QUICK BROWN FOX JUMPS OVER THE LAZY DOG

LIQUID CRYSTAL FAMILY

LIQUID CRYSTAL
LIQUID CRYSTAL
MONOSPACED

Cornel Windlin/Gilles Gavillet
Lineto
Zurich, Switzerland
1999

Liquid Crystal was based on a set of complex modules, from which all the letterforms were generated. The typeface has two versions, one spaced and slightly kerned, the other monospaced so all parts of the module stay exactly in position.

LIQUID CRYSTAL

NOVA MM 500 WEIGHT 500 OPTICAL

NOVA MM 500 WEIGHT 500 OPTICAL

The quick brown fox jumps over the lazy dog
THE QUICK BROWN FOX JUMPS OVER THE LAZY DOG

NOVA MM FAMILY

nova mm 0 0
nova mm 1000 0
nova mm 500 500
nova mm 0 1000
nova mm 1000 1000

David Rust
Optimo
Lausanne, Switzerland
1998

Nova MM allows the user to modify the shape and weight of the font using Multiple Master technology.

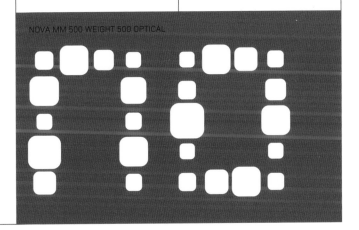

NOVA MM 500 WEIGHT 500 OPTICAL

ONE A.M.

ONE A.M.

AaBbCcDdEeFfGgHhIi
JjKkLlMmNnOoPpQqRr
SsTtUuVvWwXxYyZz
1234567890

ONE A.M.

The quick brown fox jumps over the lazy dog
THE QUICK BROWN FOX JUMPS OVER THE LAZY DOG

ONE A.M. FAMILY

One A.M.

Tnop Wangsillapakun
T–26 Digital Type Foundry
Chicago, US
1999

One A.M. was originally designed for
a stock photography book containing
images of the United States.

ONE A.M.

PRESET-B

PRESET

AaBbCcDdEeFfGgHhIi
JjKkLlMmNnOoPpQqRr
SsTtUuVvWwXxYyZz
1234567890

PRESET-B

The quick brown fox jumps over the lazy dog
THE QUICK BROWN FOX JUMPS OVER THE LAZY DOG

PRESET FAMILY

Preset-B Ultra Light
Preset-B Light
Preset-B
Preset-C
Preset-F

Julian Morey
Club Twenty-One
London, UK
1998

Preset is a square matrix typeface family based on an electronic instrument display.

PRESET-B

SHEET 2000

SHEET 2000

The quick brown fox jumps over the lazy dog
THE QUICK BROWN FOX JUMPS OVER THE LAZY DOG

SHEET FAMILY

Sheet

Sheet 2000

Hideki Inaba
Hideki Inaba Design
Tokyo, Japan
1999/2000

Sheet 2000 is the latest version of Sheet, a typeface used in +81 magazine which was based on a 7 x 7 grid from which elements were deleted.

SHEET 2000

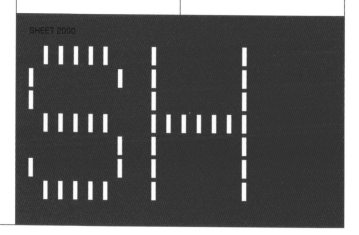

SQUARETYPE

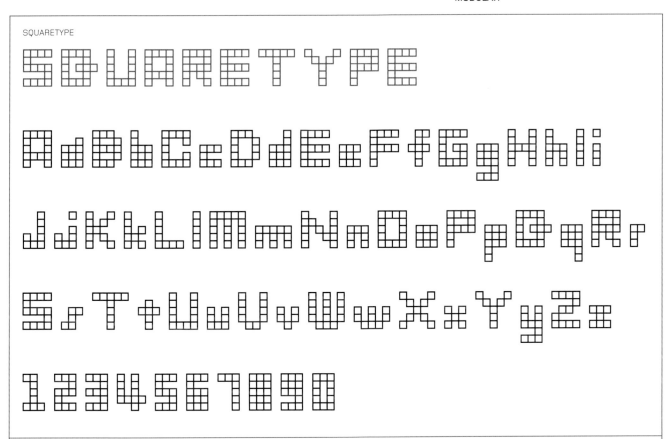

SQUARETYPE

The quick brown fox jumps over the lazy dog
THE QUICK BROWN FOX JUMPS OVER THE LAZY DOG

SQUARETYPE FAMILY

Squaretype
ァジィフゕァ゛

Nobutaka Sato
Extra Design
Sapporo, Japan
1998

Squaretype was created using a
very basic idea and structure, simply
using squares to build letterforms.

SQUARETYPE

TRICOT

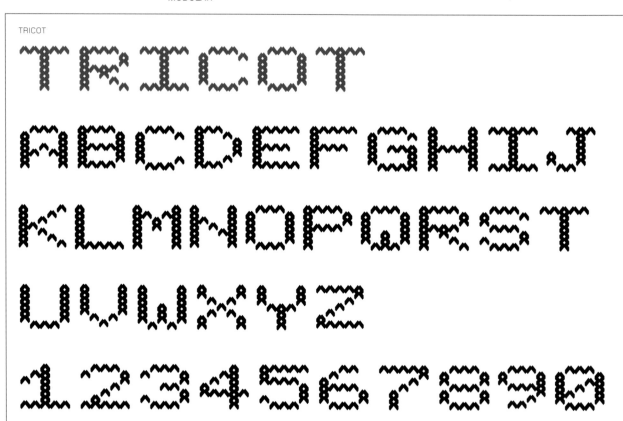

TRICOT

THE QUICK BROWN FOX JUMPS OVER THE LAZY DOG

TRICOT FAMILY

TRICOT

Kimou Meyer/Vincent Sahli
Grotesk
Geneva, Switzerland
2001

Tricot is based on the stitches of knitwear, and was enclosed on a floppy disk in the pocket of a woollen sweater as a limited edition for a fashion company.

TRICOT

UNDA CIRCLES

AaBbCcDdEeFfGgHhIiJj

KkLlMmNnOoPpQqRrSs

TtUuVvWwXxYyZz

1234567890

UNDA CIRCLES

The quick brown fox jumps over the lazy dog
THE QUICK BROWN FOX JUMPS OVER THE LAZY DOG

UNDA FAMILY

UNDA Circles
UNDA Horizontal
UNDA Square
UNDA Triangle
UNDA Vertical

Nick Hayes
Identikal Foundry
London, UK
1997

UNDA, which stands for Ultra New Design Accessory, was created to provide a wide range of fonts which allow a variety of styles within a constant grid. UNDA has around forty variations and is still growing.

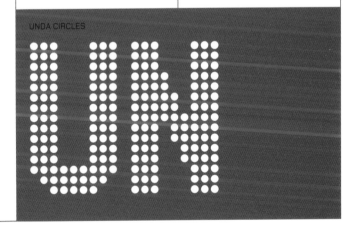

UNDA CIRCLES

AF VIDEO WALL

VIDEO WALL

ABCDEFGHIJ

KLMNOPQRST

UVWXYZ

1234567890

AF VIDEO WALL

THE QUICK BROWN FOX JUMPS OVER THE LAZY DOG

AF VIDEO WALL FAMILY

VIDEO WALL

Anthony Burrill
Acme Fonts
London, UK
1998

AF Video Wall is based on the grid of a 4 x 4 monitor video wall. Each character uses the least number of divisions of the grid. It was originally drawn as an animated sequence to be shown on the video wall of Levi's flagship store in London.

AF VIDEO WALL

ZEBUGRADES

[display of Zebugrades font characters — alphabet and numerals 1234567890]

ZEBUGRADES

[display of Zebugrades text samples]

ZEBUGRADES FAMILY

[Zebugrades]

Kano
Zetuei Fonts
Tokyo, Japan
2000

Zebugrades is a contemporary interpretation of black-letter type. It was constructed using a minimum number of elements.

ZEBUGRADES

BASIC-21

BASIC-21

AaBbCcDdEeFfGgHhIi
JjKkL1MmNnOoPpQqRr
SsTtUuVvWwXxYyZz
1234567890

BASIC-21

The quick brown fox jumps over the lazy dog
THE QUICK BROWN FOX JUMPS OVER THE LAZY DOG

BASIC-21 FAMILY

Basic-21

Julian Morey
Club Twenty-One
London, UK
2001

Basic-21 was designed specially for TYPE 1 and is free on the CD that accompanies this book. Its design pays homage to the 8-bit world of the 1980s home computer.

BASIC-21

BETA SIX

BÉTA SIX

A a B b C c D d É c F F G q H h l i J j

K k L I M m N n O o P p Q q R r

S s T t U u U u W w X x Y y Z z

1 2 3 4 5 6 7 8 9 0

BETA SIX

The quick brown fox jumps over the lazy dog
THE QUICK BROWN FOX JUMPS OVER THE LAZY DOG

BETA SIX FAMILY

Beta Six

Jonathan Hitchen
Beaufonts
Manchester, UK
2001

Beta Six is part of an ongoing experiment to create a family of fonts with a maximum height of six pixels, at screen resolution of 72dpi, for both upper- and lowercase.

BETA SIX

CROSS OUT REGULAR

CROSS OUT REGULAR

THE QUICK BROWN FOX JUMPS OVER THE LAZY DOG

CROSS FAMILY

CROSS REGULAR
CROSS BOLD
CROSS OUT REGULAR
CROSS OUT BOLD

Nathan Gale
Brighton, UK
2000

Cross was designed for use specifically within Creative Review magazine. It is a bitmapped version of the typeface CR Gothic designed by Robin Nicholas.

CROSS OUT REGULAR

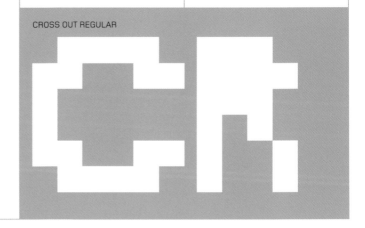

FF EBOY EXTENDED BETA

AaBbCOdEEFFG9

HhIiJiLlMMNNOPQ9

RrrSTtUuVWWXYZ

1234567890

FF EBOY EXTENDED BETA

The quick brown fox jumps over the lazy dog
THE QUICK BROWN FOX JUMPS OVER THE LAZY DOG

FF EBOY FAMILY

Eboy Gamma

Eboy Beta

Eboy Alpha

Eboy Extended Gamma

Eboy Extended Beta

Eboy Extended Alpha

Eboy TNT Gamma

Eboy TNT Beta

Eboy TNT Alpha

Kai Vermehr
eBoy
FSI FontShop International
Berlin, Germany
1999

FF Eboy is based on the geometry of pixeled screen fonts and was created specially for use on screen and on the web. Each variation is available in three weights, or resolutions, based on grids of five, seven and nine pixels.

FF EBOY EXTENDED BETA

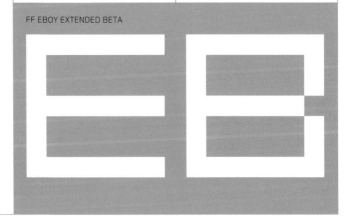

ELECTRO

ELECTRO

ELECTRO FAMILY

Electro-P
Electro

Julian Morey
Club Twenty-One
London, UK
2000

Electro was inspired by a book
about the early development of the
barcode. The letterforms are based
on grid pattern tests in the book.

ELECTRO

HYPERTEXTURION 1.0

HYPERTEXTURION

Aa Bb Cc Dd Ee Ff Gg Hh Ii
Jj Kk Ll Mm Nn Oo Pp Qq Rr
Ss Tt Uu Vv Ww Xx Yy Zz
1234567890

HYPERTEXTURION 1.0

The quick brown fox jumps over the lazy dog
THE QUICK BROWN FOX JUMPS OVER THE LAZY DOG

HYPERTEXTURION FAMILY

Hypertexturion 1.0
Hypertexturion 1.1

Matius Gerardo Grieck
[+ism]
London, UK
2000

Hypertexturion is based on 12th- and 13th-century gothic scripts. It merges early forms of angular calligraphy into a 21st-century digital bitmap font.

HYPERTEXTURION 1.0

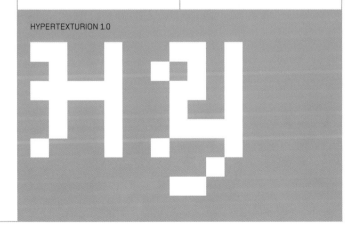

AF SATELLITE

AF SATELLITE

THE QUICK BROWN FOX JUMPS OVER THE LAZY. DOG

AF SATELLITE FAMILY

SATELLITE

Christian Küsters
Acme Fonts
London, UK
1998

AF Satellite's overall design principle was to eliminate formal choice. It was based on a system where the designer established an initial set of rules and then allowed the form of the typeface to be determined by those rules.

AF SATELLITE

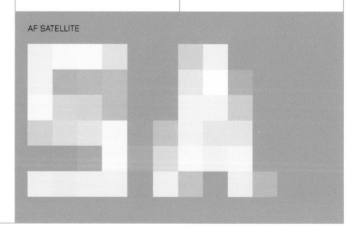

SLIVER LIGHT

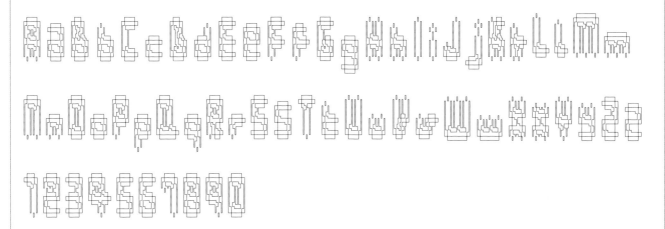

SLIVER LIGHT

The quick brown fox jumps over the lazy dog
THE QUICK BROWN FOX JUMPS OVER THE LAZY DOG

SLIVER FAMILY

Sliver Light

Sliver Heavy

Megumu Kasuga
London, UK
1998

Sliver was initially drawn as a
simple and legible typeface using
only straight lines. It was further
developed using a system of
repeatedly cutting, copying and
pasting elements from the
original letterforms.

SLIVER LIGHT

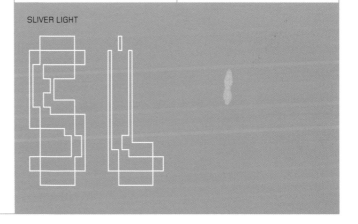

TYPIX

TYPIX

ABCDEFGHIJKLM
NOPQRSTUVWXYZ
1234567890

TYPIX

THE QUICK BROWN FOX JUMPS OVER THE LAZY DOG

TYPIX FAMILY

TYPIX

Simon Sankarayya
Digit
London, UK
2000

Typix is an aliased font created for the redesign of the Creative Review magazine CD-Rom. Its functional and formulaic design was in keeping with the overall design of the interface.

TYPIX

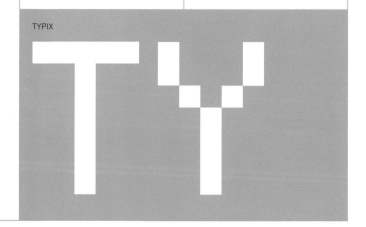

VERTICE ORTHO LIGHT

VERTICE

ABCDEFGHIJK
LMNOPQRSTU
VWXYZ
1234567890

VERTICE ORTHO LIGHT

THE QUICK BROWN FOX JUMPS OVER THE LAZY DOG

VERTICE FAMILY

ORTHO LIGHT
ORTHO REGULAR
ORTHO BOLD
ORTHO OUTLINE
28MM BOLD
28MM OUTLINE
28MM RIGHT
28MM RIGHT OUTLINE
28MM LEFT
28MM LEFT OUTLINE
35MM BOLD
35MM OUTLINE
35MM LEFT
35MM LEFT OUTLINE
35MM RIGHT
35MM RIGHT OUTLINE

Spencer Higgins
Threecolor
New York, US
2001

Vertice is a study of simple letterforms shaped by shifting perspectives. It was generated using a 3D application to change the focal length and position of the camera, thereby creating a family of typefaces.

VERTICE ORTHO LIGHT

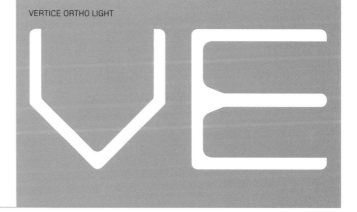

WHITE

WHITE

ABCDEFGHIJKLMN
OPQRSTUVWXYZ
1234567890

WHITE

THE QUICK BROWN FOX JUMPS OVER THE LAZY DOG

WHITE FAMILY

WHITE

Alexander Gelman/David Heasty
Design Machine
New York, US
2000

White was intended to be used in both print and web applications. Set at 21pt it functions as a perfectly readable typeface for screen use, and in print its three-dimensional rendering creates an excellent typographic texture.

WHITE

FF XCREEN DOUBLE

XCREEN

AaBbCcDdEeFfGgHhIi
JjKkLlMmNnOoPpQqRr
SsTtUuVvWwXxYyZz
1234567890

FF XCREEN DOUBLE

The quick brown fox jumps over the lazy dog
THE QUICK BROWN FOX JUMPS OVER THE LAZY DOG

FF XCREEN FAMILY

Xcreen Straight
Xcreen Double
Xcreen Linex

Kai Vermehr
eBoy
FSI FontShop International
Berlin, Germany
1999

FF Xcreen was developed to create
a screen font with minimum height.
The Straight version of FF Xcreen is
optimized for 7pt/72dpi, the Linex
and Double versions are 14pt/72dpi.

FF XCREEN DOUBLE

CONTACT INDEX: DESIGNERS

Achim Reichert
achim@vier5.de
www.vier5.de

Adrian Talbot
adriant@intro-uk.com
www.intro-uk.com

Alessio Leonardi
info@fontshop.com
www.fontshop.com

Alexander Gelman
gelman@designmachine.net
www.designmachine.net

Andrew Smith
info@2rebels.com
www.2rebels.com

Angus R. Shamal
info@arstype.com
www.arstype.com

Anne Wehebrink
acme@chkdesign.demon.co.uk
www.acmefonts.net

Anthony Burrill
anthony@friendchip.com
www.anthonyburrill.com

Arjen Noordeman
arjen@noordeman.com
www.noordeman.com

Austin Cowdall
fonts@new-online.co.uk
www.new-online.co.uk

Barry Deck
fontmaster@3st2.com
www.thirstype.com

Ben Drury
drury@easynet.co.uk

Brode Vosloo
brode@sacrednipple.co.za
www.sacrednipple.co.za

Carlos Segura
info@t26.com
www.t26.com

Chester
fontmaster@3st2.com
www.thirstype.com

Christian Küsters
acme@chkdesign.demon.co.uk
www.acmefonts.net

Christian Schwartz
info@fontbureau.com
www.fontbureau.com

Claudio Piccinini
fontmaster@3st2.com
www.thirstype.com

Cornel Windlin
info@lineto.com
www.lineto.com

David Crow
david.crow1@which.net

David Heasty
david@designmachine.net
www.designmachine.net

David Quay
mail@foundrytypes.co.uk
www.thefoundrystudio.co.uk
www.foundrytypes.co.uk

David Rust
service@optimo.ch
www.optimo.ch

Florian Heiss
cowboy@scheufler-heiss.com
www.scheufler-heiss.com

Freda Sack
mail@foundrytypes.co.uk
www.thefoundrystudio.co.uk
www.foundrytypes.co.uk

Gareth Hague
gareth@dqjaltd.co.uk

Gilles Gavillet
service@optimo.ch
www.optimo.ch

Gregg Brokaw
fontmaster@3st2.com
www.thirstype.com

Gregor Schönborn
gregor@copy.li
www.copy.li

Henrik Kubel
info@a2-graphics.co.uk
www.a2-graphics.co.uk
www.fontyoufonts.com

Hideki Inaba
inaba@t3.rim.or.jp

Ian Mitchell
info@beaufonts.com
www.beaufonts.com

Jakob Straub
jakob.straub@gmx.ch
www.jakobstraub.com

James Glover
drop@fluidesign.co.uk
www.fluidesign.co.uk

James Goggin
info@lineto.com
www.lineto.com

Jeremy Tankard
jtankard@typography.net
www.typography.net

John Randle
info@agentfriction.com

Jonas Williamson
info@lineto.com
www.lineto.com

Jonathan Hitchen
info@beaufonts.com
www.beaufonts.com

Julian Morey
info@typeclub.co.uk
www.typeclub.co.uk

Kai Vermehr
info@fontshop.com
www.fontshop.com

Kano
info@zetuei.com
www.zetuei.com

Kimou Meyer
info@grotesk.to
www.grotesk.to

Laurence Jaccottet
laurence@copy.li
www.copy.li

Laurent Benner
info@lineto.com
www.lineto.com

Lee Basford
drop@fluidesign.co.uk
www.fluidesign.co.uk

Lee Fasciani
leef@intro-uk.com
www.intro-uk.com

Lopetz
bd@bermuda.ch
www.burodestruct.net
www.typedifferent.com

Malte Haust
contact@bionic-systems.com
www.bionic-systems.com

Martha Stuttergger
info@lineto.com
www.lineto.com

Masahiko Nakamura
info@lineto.com
www.lineto.com

Masayuki Sato
sato@mks.jp.org
www.mks.jp.org

Matius Gerardo Grieck
a90037tm@plusism.com
www.plusism.com

Matt Wingfield
matt.wingfield@virgin.net

MBrunner
bd@bermuda.ch
www.burodestruct.net
www.typedifferent.com

Megumu Kasuga
meg-kasuga@yahoo.co.jp

Mike Essl
mike@choppingblock.com
www.choppingblock.com

Mike Kohnke
mike@weassociated.com
www.weassociated.com

Miles Newlyn
info@x-and-y.co.uk
www.x-and-y.co.uk

Mitch
mitchy.bwoy@virgin.net

Neville Brody
info@researchstudios.com
www.researchstudios.com

Nick Hayes
info@identikal.co.uk
www.identikal.com

Nico Schweizer
info@lineto.com
www.lineto.com

Niels Wehrspann
niels@copy.li
www.copy.li

Nobutaka Sato
info@extra.jp.org
www.extra.jp.org

Pablo Medina
fonts@plazm.com
www.plazm.com

Patrick Giasson
fontmaster@3st2.com
www.thirstype.com

Paul Sych
fontmaster@3st2.com
www.thirstype.com

Rian Hughes
rianhughes@aol.com
www.devicefonts.co.uk

Rick Valicenti
fontmaster@3st2.com
www.thirstype.com

Robert Green
rob@i-bz.com
www.i-bz.com

Robin Nicholas
enquire.europe@agfamonotype.com
www.agfamonotype.co.uk

Rodrigo Cavazos
info@psyops.com
www.psyops.com

Sandy Suffield
acme@chkdesign.demon.co.uk
www.acmefonts.net

Scott Williams
info@a2-graphics.co.uk
www.a2-graphics.co.uk
www.fontyoufonts.com

Sebastian Lester
sebastian.lester@agfamonotype.com
www.agfamonotype.co.uk

Sheila Dorje
sheila@ct.oj.co.za
www.oj.co.za

Shin Sasaki
info@extra.jp.org
www.extra.jp.org

Simon Gofton
info@hingston.net

Simon Sankarayya
sanky@digitlondon.com
www.digitlondon.com

Spencer Higgins
spencer@threecolor.com
www.threecolor.com

Stephan Mueller
info@lineto.com
www.lineto.com

Stephane Delgado
service@optimo.ch
www.optimo.ch

Swifty
swifty@swifty.co.uk
www.swifty.co.uk

Tim Fletcher
info@typical.co.uk

Timothy Donaldson
info@fontshop.com
www.fontshop.com

Tnop Wangsillapakun
tnop@tnop.com
www.tnop.com

Tobias Frere-Jones
www.typography.com

Tom Hingston
info@hingston.net

Tomi Haaparanta
info@protokid.net
www.protokid.net

Tomo Takeue
tomo@tomotomo.net
www.tomotomo.net

Tyler Askew
t-askew@bellsouth.net
www.mindspring.com/~askewh/

Urs Lehni
info@lineto.com
www.lineto.com

Vincent Sahli
info@grotesk.to
www.grotesk.to

Wayne Thompson
ilene.strizver@itcfonts.com
www.itcfonts.com

Wolfgang Breuer
wbreuer@mittlerekoernung.de
www.forhomeorofficeuse.com

Yaki Molcho
rutyaki@vital.co.il

CONTACT INDEX: COMPANIES/FOUNDRIES

//copy//
info@copy.li
www.copy.li

2Rebels
info@2rebels.com
www.2rebels.com

A2-Graphics/SW/HK
info@a2-graphics.co.uk
www.a2-graphics.co.uk
www.fontyoufonts.com

Acme Fonts
acme@chkdesign.demon.co.uk
www.acmefonts.net

AGFA Monotype
enquire.europe@agfamonotype.com
info@agfamonotype.com
www.agfamonotype.co.uk
www.fonts.com

Alias
gareth@dqjaltd.co.uk

ARS Type
info@arstype.com
www.arstype.com

Beaufonts
info@beaufonts.com
www.beaufonts.com

Bionic Systems
contact@bionic-systems.com
www.bionic-systems.com

Büro Destruct
bd@bermuda.ch
www.burodestruct.net
www.typedifferent.com

Club Twenty-One
info@typeclub.co.uk
www.typeclub.co.uk

Design Machine
info@designmachine.net
www.designmachine.net

Device
rianhughes@aol.com
www.devicefonts.co.uk

Digit
sanky@digitlondon.com
www.digitlondon.com

eBoy
contact@eboy.com
www.eboy.com

Elektrosmog
info@lineto.com
www.lineto.com

Emigre Inc.
info@emigre.com
www.emigre.com

Extra Design
info@extra.jp.org
www.extra.jp.org

Fluid
drop@fluidesign.co.uk
www.fluidesign.co.uk

Font Bureau
info@fontbureau.com
www.fontbureau.com

ForHomeOrOfficeUse
all@forhomeorofficeuse.com
www.forhomeorofficeuse.com

Fountain
info@fountain.nu
www.fountain.nu

FSI FontShop International
info@fontshop.com
www.fontshop.com

GarageFonts
info@garagefonts.com
www.garagefonts.com

Grotesk
info@grotesk.to
www.grotesk.to

House Industries
andycruz@houseind.com
www.houseindustries.com

Identikal Foundry
info@identikal.co.uk
www.identikal.com

International Typeface Corporation
ilene.strizver@itcfonts.com
www.itcfonts.com

Intro
intro@intro-uk.com
www.intro-uk.com

Lineto
info@lineto.com
www.lineto.com

Maniackers Design
sato@mks.jp.org
www.mks.jp.org

Mittlere Körnung
wbreuer@mittlerekoernung.de
www.mittlerekoernung.de

NEW
fonts@new-online.co.uk
www.new-online.co.uk

Norm
nrm@norm.to
www.norm.to

Optimo
service@optimo.ch
www.optimo.ch

Orange Juice Design
juice@oj.co.za
www.oj.co.za

Plazm Fonts
fonts@plazm.com
www.plazm.com

Protokid
info@protokid.net
www.protokid.net

Psy/Ops Type Foundry
info@psyops.com
www.psyops.com

Scheufler & Heiss
cowboy@scheufler-heiss.com
www.scheufler-heiss.com

Swifty Typografix
swifty@swifty.co.uk
www.swifty.co.uk

T-26 Digital Type Foundry
info@t26.com
www.t26.com

The Chopping Block Inc.
info@choppingblock.com
www.choppingblock.com

The Foundry
mail@foundrytypes.co.uk
www.thefoundrystudio.co.uk
www.foundrytypes.co.uk

Thirstype
fontmaster@3st2.com
www.thirstype.com

Threecolor
spencer@threecolor.com
www.threecolor.com

tomotomo.net
tomo@tomotomo.net
www.tomotomo.net

Typical
info@typical.co.uk

Vier5
hallo@vier5.de
www.vier5.de

We Associated: Type
mike@weassociated.com
www.weassociated.com

x&y
info@x-and-y.co.uk
www.x-and-y.co.uk

Zetuei Fonts
info@zetuei.com
www.zetuei.com

[+ism]
a90037tm@plusism.com
www.plusism.com

SUBMISSIONS FORM

■ ALL TYPEFACE SUBMISSIONS MUST HAVE BEEN DESIGNED FROM 2001 ONWARDS
■ INCLUDE A FONT SPECIMEN WITH EACH TYPEFACE PROVIDED
■ FILL OUT A NEW SUBMISSIONS FORM WITH EACH TYPEFACE FAMILY SUBMITTED

NAME OF DESIGNER

COMPANY

CITY   COUNTRY

TEL   FAX

EMAIL   WEBSITE

NAME OF TYPEFACE/FAMILY

FOUNDRY/FOUNDRIES

YEAR OF TYPEFACE DESIGN

CLASSIFICATION OF TYPEFACE

DESCRIPTION OF TYPEFACE

■ PLEASE SIGN THE DECLARATION BELOW

I confirm that I have the right to grant permission for the work listed above to be reproduced in the book TYPE 2 to be published by Laurence King Publishing Ltd in the UK and by other publishers worldwide and that all copyrights have been cleared for this purpose (world rights, all languages). I accept that no fee is payable by the submitter or the publisher, or to or by any third parties in respect of the work published.

SIGNED   DATE

NAME

■ PLEASE RETURN TO NATHAN GALE

MAIL 12-26 LEXINGTON STREET, LONDON W1R 4HQ, UNITED KINGDOM **FAX** +44 20 7970 6712 **EMAIL** NATHANG@CENTAUR.CO.UK